Spider-Man: Into the Spider-Verse

Exploring the dynamic genres of animation and comic book films, this book examines the hypertextual design of *Spider-Man: Into the Spider-Verse* (2018) and its critical involvement in attempts to diversify representations in youth-oriented cinema and culture.

Several years after the movie's immense commercial and critical success, a look back on the innovative features of *Spider-Man: Into the Spider-Verse* shows how the film's force derives from its thoughtful depiction of Miles Morales – a young, Afro-Latino superhero who must face systemic obstacles his white predecessor never worried about. Engaging a web of pressing topics in the field – from transmedia storytelling to identity formation and minority representation – this book offers an accessible analysis of the citational and animation techniques that help this film to sensitively confront the combustible dynamics of racial representation in contemporary American culture.

Written in an approachable style, this book is suitable for undergraduates, postgraduates, and specialists in the field. It is a versatile resource for media studies, film studies, animation studies, and cultural studies courses, but will also appeal to fans seeking to investigate the thematic underbelly of *Into the Spider-Verse*.

Charlie Michael is Assistant Professor in the Department of Film and Media at Emory University. His research focuses on popular culture and media industries in a global context. He is the author of *French Blockbusters: Cultural Politics of a Transnational Cinema* (2019) and the co-editor of the *Directory of World Cinema: France* (2013), and his work has also appeared in journals such as *SubStance*, *Transnational Screens*, and *The Velvet Light Trap*.

Cinema and Youth Cultures

Series Editors: Siân Lincoln and Yannis Tzioumakis

Cinema and Youth Cultures engages with well-known youth films from American cinema as well as the cinemas of other countries. Using a variety of methodological and critical approaches the series volumes provide informed accounts of how young people have been represented in film, while also exploring the ways in which young people engage with films made for and about them. In doing this, the Cinema and Youth Cultures series contributes to important and long-standing debates about youth cultures, how these are mobilized and articulated in influential film texts and the impact that these texts have had on popular culture at large.

American Graffiti
George Lucas, the New Hollywood and the Baby Boom Generation
Peter Krämer

Before Sunrise
Young Love on the Move
María del Mar Azcona and Celestino Deleyto

Rock around the Clock
Exploitation, Rock 'n' Roll and the Origins of Youth Culture
Yannis Tzioumakis and Siân Lincoln

Spider-Man: Into the Spider-Verse
Youth, Race, and the Hypertext
Charlie Michael

For more information about this series, please visit: https://www.routledge.com/Cinema-and-Youth-Cultures/book-series/CYC

Spider-Man: Into the Spider-Verse
Youth, Race, and the Hypertext

Charlie Michael

Taylor & Francis Group

LONDON AND NEW YORK

First published 2025
by Routledge
4 Park Square, Milton Park, Abingdon, Oxon OX14 4RN

and by Routledge
605 Third Avenue, New York, NY 10158

Routledge is an imprint of the Taylor & Francis Group, an informa business

British Library Cataloguing-in-Publication Data
A catalogue record for this book is available from the British Library

Library of Congress Cataloging-in-Publication Data
Names: Michael, Charlie, author.
Title: Spider-Man, into the Spider-Verse : youth, race, and the hypertext / Charlie Michael.
Description: Abingdon, Oxon ; New York, NY : Routledge, 2025. | Series: Cinema and youth cultures | Includes bibliographical references and index.
Identifiers: LCCN 2024007918 (print) | LCCN 2024007919 (ebook) | ISBN 9780367764500 (hardback) | ISBN 9780367764524 (paperback) | ISBN 9781003166962 (ebook)
Subjects: LCSH: Spider-Man, into the Spider-Verse (Motion picture) | Spider-Man (Fictitious character) | Motion pictures–Social aspects–United States–History–21st century. | LCGFT: Film criticism.
Classification: LCC PN1997.2.S6935 M53 2025 (print) | LCC PN1997.2.S6935 (ebook) | DDC 791.43/72–dc23/eng/20240329
LC record available at https://lccn.loc.gov/2024007918
LC ebook record available at https://lccn.loc.gov/2024007919

ISBN: 978-0-367-76450-0 (hbk)
ISBN: 978-0-367-76452-4 (pbk)
ISBN: 978-1-003-16696-2 (ebk)

DOI: 10.4324/9781003166962

Typeset in Times New Roman
by Taylor & Francis Books

For Jeevan & Avishan

Contents

Figures

Series Editors' Introduction

Despite the high visibility of youth films in the global media marketplace, especially since the 1980s when Conglomerate Hollywood realized that such films were not only strong box office performers but also the starting point for ancillary sales in other media markets as well as for franchise building, academic studies that focused specifically on such films were slow to materialize. Arguably the most important factor behind academia's reluctance to engage with youth films was a (then) widespread perception within the Film and Media Studies communities that such films held little cultural value and significance, and therefore were not worthy of serious scholarly research and examination. Just like the young subjects they represented, whose interests and cultural practices have been routinely deemed transitional and transitory, so were the films that represented them perceived as fleeting and easily digestible, destined to be forgotten quickly, as soon as the next youth film arrived in cinema screens a week later.

Under these circumstances, and despite a small number of pioneering studies in the 1980s and early 1990s, the field of 'youth film studies' did not really start blossoming and attracting significant scholarly attention until the 2000s and in combination with similar developments in cognate areas such as 'girl studies'. However, because of the paucity of material in the previous decades, the majority of these new studies in the 2000s focused primarily on charting the field and therefore steered clear of long, in-depth examinations of youth films or was exemplified by edited collections that chose particular films to highlight certain issues to the detriment of others. In other words, despite providing often wonderfully rich accounts of youth cultures as these have been captured by key films, these studies could not possibly dedicate sufficient space to engage with more than just a few key aspects of youth films.

In more recent (post-2010) years, a number of academic studies started delimiting their focus and therefore providing more space for in-depth examinations of key types of youth films, such as slasher films and biker films or examining youth films in particular historical periods. From that point on, it was a matter of time for the first publications that focused exclusively on key youth films from a number of perspectives to appear (*Mamma Mia! The Movie, Twilight* and *Dirty Dancing* are among the first films to receive this treatment). Conceived primarily as edited collections, these studies provided a multifaceted analysis of these films, focusing on such issues as the politics of representing youth, the stylistic and narrative choices that characterize these films and the extent to which they are representative of a youth cinema, the ways these films address their audiences, the ways youth audiences engage with these films, the films' industrial location and other relevant issues.

It is within this increasingly maturing and expanding academic environment that the **Cinema and Youth Cultures** volumes arrive, aiming to consolidate existing knowledge, provide new perspectives, apply innovative methodological approaches, offer sustained and in-depth analyses of key films and therefore become the 'go to' resource for students and scholars interested in theoretically informed, author-itative accounts of youth cultures in film. As editors, we have tried to be as inclusive as possible in our selection of key examples of youth films by commissioning volumes on films that span the history of cinema, including the silent film era; that portray contemporary youth cultures as well as ones associated with particular historical periods; that represent examples of mainstream and independent cinema; that originate in American cinema and the cinemas of other nations; that attracted significant critical attention and commercial success during their initial release and that were 'rediscovered' after an unpromising initial critical reception. Together these volumes are going to advance youth film studies while also being able to offer extremely detailed examinations of films that are now considered significant contributions to cinema and our cultural life more broadly.

We hope readers will enjoy the series.

Siân Lincoln & Yannis Tzioumakis
Cinema & Youth Cultures Series Editors

Acknowledgements

This book would not exist in any universe without the support of many people in this one.

Thank you to the collective, creative consciousness of the team at Sony Pictures Animation, who made a rare movie I never tire of watching. Usually when I write about a film, I want to take a break from it for a long time. I may actually rewatch *The Spider-Verse* tonight.

Thank you to the good people at Routledge and the 'Cinema and Youth Cultures' series editors, Yannis Tzoumakis and Siân Lincoln. Yannis especially has been a source of encouragement over the past few years, never wavering in his support for my work even as deadlines came and went.

Thank you to Georgia Gwinnett College, to my students there, and to my colleagues in the recently founded Department of Visual and Performing Arts (VAPA). They provided more moral support than they could possibly know by simply asking for – and listening to – my occasional updates on this project over the past few years. Kate Balsley in particular has provided a sympathetic ear on numerous occasions.

Thank you to my various colleagues in the field of film and media at-large. Two graduate school friends from Wisconsin-Madison, Mark Minett and Brad Schauer, offered a bushel of materials to kickstart my initial research into comics and superheroes. Since our panel at SCMS 2021, Russell Meeuf, Ayanni Hanna, and Eve Benhamou have also helped stoke my passion for untangling *The Spider-Verse*.

Thank you to the numerous comics, superhero, and Spider-Man die-hards who have helped light my path these last few years. These include Sridhar Pappu, to whom I owe almost all of my early childhood exposure to superheroes, and Chad Anderson, who offered welcome guidance at the beginning of the project. They also include Chris, Jamie, and the rest of their warmly enthusiastic staff at Infinite Realities, who nourish the imaginations of numerous Atlanta teens, but also never tire of answering naïve questions from those of us who are perennially 'in' (but no longer 'of') the youth cultures that their wonderful store exists to serve.

Thank you to Taylor McGhee, who has helped me to see and articulate crucial new dimensions of the film over the years, first as my student at Emory in a course on transmedia, and then as the host of her podcast on multiracial identities.

Thank you to my family – my parents, Jim and Sarah; my sisters, Katie and Eleanor; my mother in-law, Chandranee; my brothers in-law, Dinesh, Joey, Keith, and Nav. The patience, encouragement, and generosity of these people – who have listened to my ideas for decades – is one of the reasons I can keep writing books like this.

Thank you to Subha, my soul mate, my intellectual companion, the love of my life. Her courage and brilliance have given me the confidence to write about topics I never would have dared touch in the past.

And finally, thank you to my dear children, Jeevan and Avishan. Their excitement in watching – and re-watching – Miles Morales, and in sharing the joy of this movie with me, has been the very life source of this project. I wrote it for them.

Introduction
'My name is Miles Morales'

Spider-Man: Into the Spider-Verse (Bob Perischetti, Peter Ramsey, and Rodney Rothman, 2018) tells the story of Miles Morales (Shameik Moore), a 13-year-old kid from Brooklyn who discovers he has super-powers after getting bitten by a radioactive spider. Like other versions of this familiar tale, Miles is an unassuming teenager; unlike other versions, he is a multiracial person of color – the only child of Rio Morales (Lauren Vélez), a Puerto Rican nurse, and Jefferson Davis (Brian Tyree Henry), a somewhat-ironically named Black police officer.

There are other notable differences. This time around, the spider gets the young hero in a different way than he does Peter Parker. Late at night in the subway, Miles is bitten while creating street art alongside his uncle, Aaron Davis (Mahershala Ali), a graffiti artist and his father's ne'er do well brother. Perhaps most importantly, even after the spider bite, Miles still has no reason to think he will ever be a super-hero. He knows that Spider-Man already exists in his world. That changes quickly though, as he witnesses Parker (Chris Pine) tragically killed while trying to stop The Kingpin (Liev Schrieber) from using his 'Super Collider' to collapse the space-time continuum. With Parker suddenly gone, no one is left to defend Brooklyn and the world from existential peril. New York needs a new masked hero – and Miles Morales will be the new Spider-Man!

In another world, *The Spider-Verse* (as this book will refer to the film for brevity's sake) could easily have become 'just another' Spider-Man movie. In many ways, it still is. Released by Columbia Pictures and Sony Pictures Entertainment in December 2018, the film is a pro-duction of Sony Pictures Animation, which at the time of the film's release was a relatively low-profile outfit – at least compared to its competition, animation juggernauts like Pixar and DreamWorks. This was especially the case since Sony Animation's past successes with films like *Cloudy with a Chance of Meatballs* (Phil Lord and Christopher

DOI: 10.4324/9781003166962-1

Miller, 2009) had been muted by a more recent run of forgettable, poorly received titles like *The Emoji Movie* (Tony Leondis, Eric Siegel, and Mike White, 2017) and *The Star* (Timothy Reckert, 2017). At the outset, *The Spider-Verse*'s somewhat confusing status also derived from its superhero's sheer popularity and from the ongoing, complicated licensing agreements involving him. As co-producer Miller put it, recalling an initial conversation with Sony executive Amy Pascal – 'At first, I thought, "Maybe there have already been a lot of Spider-Man movies?"' ('The Secrets Behind *Spider-Man* ...' 2019).

For this new film, Sony worked 'in association with' Marvel Studios, thereby sharing some corporate personnel but maintaining separate ownership rights. And despite Sony's autonomy, that 'association' did have creative consequences. For instance, early versions of *The Spider-Verse* script featured Ganke Lee, Miles' Korean-American childhood friend who plays a major supporting role in the comics, as well as Jason Reynolds' subsequent youth novel adaptation, *Miles Morales: Spider-Man* (2017). However, when the release of *Spider-Man: Homecoming* (Jon Watts, 2017) revealed the inclusion of Ned Leeds (Jacob Batalon) as a roommate and comedic foil for Peter (Tom Holland), the *Spider-Verse* screenplay was revised, removing Ganke to avoid redundancy or confusion (Bui 2019). Parallels like this gave *The Spider-Verse* a confusing aura as a sort of creative satellite to *Homecoming*, which established Holland as the new leading Spider-Man of the Marvel Cinematic Universe (MCU) – following in the footsteps of Tobey Maguire of *Spider-Man 1* (Sam Raimi, 2002), *2* (Raimi, 2004) and *3* (Raimi, 2007), and Andrew Garfield of *The Amazing Spider-Man 1* (Marc Webb, 2012) and *2* (Webb, 2014).

All this to say that Miles and his *Spider-Verse* could easily have swung much further under the radar. Fortunately, the film – which otherwise might have just resurfaced on 'Family Entertainment' queues a few months after its run – emerged as one of the biggest critical and commercial successes of 2018. Building on gradual buzz and word of mouth, it eclipsed a respectable $375 million at the box office (including its international run), and became the first superhero film to win an Oscar for Best Animated Feature the following year.[1] Since then, the film's reputation has only grown, and five years on it is a title adored by fans and critics alike – routinely listed at the top of ranking lists for the genre as a whole.[2] Among its legions of adoring supporters, many are aficionados who know the genre quite intimately. They include high profile geek-auteurs like *Guardians of the Galaxy* (2014) director and comic enthusiast James Gunn, who calls it 'the best superhero movie ever made' ('James Gunn ...' 2023) and noted podcaster and Spider-

Man expert Dan Gvozden, who despite boasting a collection of every Spider-Man comic book ever released, confesses a special admiration for Miles and his story as presented in the film, which he credits with giving him the courage to finally become a father ('Spider-Man: Across...' 2023). Meanwhile, among animation lovers on YouTube and elsewhere, *The Spider-Verse* is now widely cited as a film that 'changed everything' in an industry overrun by Pixar-style photo-realist rendering, bringing back a variety of 2D and hand-drawn techniques to the tools of computer graphic imagery (CGI).

Finally, cultural critics also widely laud the film for its sensitive portrayal of Miles, that rare character of color whose on-screen experiences somehow ring both authentic and universal, as if to prove that his closing mantra – 'anyone can wear the mask' – can be more than just the stuff of fictitious hyperbole. At the time of writing, the first *Spider-Verse* now stands as the flagship title in its own blockbuster franchise, with a critically acclaimed sequel, *Across the Spider-Verse* (Joaquim Dos Santos, Kemp Powers, and Justin K. Thompson, 2023), and a third film – *Beyond the Spider-Verse* – reportedly on the way in 2024. In just its first two weeks, *Across the Spider-Verse* grossed over $300 million at the domestic box office, outpacing the entire international run of the original.[3] Rather than fade into an oblivion of Spider-fatigue, this obscure animated feature – with its title that resembles an academic conference paper more than a blockbuster – seems to have conquered Hollywood, resetting the agenda for superhero films, animation techniques, and racial representation in popular culture.

Beginning this account by entertaining these alternative fates also seems appropriate for a title emblematic of the pluralistic narrative tendencies of contemporary American popular culture. Multiverses like the one depicted in *The Spider-Verse* seem to be the order of the day in early 2020s Hollywood – a tendency that gained even more critical legitimacy with the Best Picture victory of the quirkily multiversal *Everything Everywhere All at Once* (Daniel Kwan and Daniel Scheinart, 2022) at the 2023 Oscars. As the latest way for franchises to provide audiences with numerous ways to see their beloved characters, multiverses provide studios with a tantalizing strategy for monetization, allowing for numerous story arcs while managing possible contradictions among them through a master conceit. Yet even against a backdrop so flush with transmedia worldbuilding – from *Star Wars*, to *Harry Potter* and the MCU, among others – *The Spider-Verse* stands out for the audacity with which it embraces and internalizes its own multiplicity. From the jump, the film proposes a sort of thought experiment for its audience, guiding them on a collective journey into various permutations of the Spider-Possible.

The multiverse idea is so central to the film's premise – so overt in its trailers and ad campaigns – that even those viewers somehow unacquainted with superhero films or fantasy genres can understand that going *into* this Spider-Verse means shedding usual expectations for stylistic and narrative continuity. As Peter B. Parker (Jake Johnson) puts it in one of the trailers, 'This could literally not get any weirder'. What this also means, of course, is that those same audiences have a chance to embrace a multiracial Spider-Man and the uplifting message of his story. Here is a film that proposes to us the possibility of an Afro-Latino teenager who becomes *the* hero of a film without automatic recourse to canonical gatekeeping. As *Spider-Verse* co-director Peter Ramsey, who became the first Black director to win an animation Oscar for his work on the film, puts it: 'People of color want to be part of the story, want to be part of the myth. If you can't be part of a myth like that, then what do you have in a culture?' (quoted in Bowman and Garcia-Navarro 2019).

With these dynamics in mind, this book scrutinizes various strategies by which *The Spider-Verse* manages to walk a high-wire act – appealing to a 'universalist' myth of American youth culture while also honoring the concerns of populations for too long excluded from that same myth. No doubt, the film's formal exercises in revising Spider-Man arrive at a particularly sensitive moment. Replacing Peter Parker with Miles Morales means flying in the face of decades of Spider-Man lore, taking on canonical gatekeepers who are more invested in the chronology of a (white) character than in any concern with equitable representation. More importantly, it means crafting a new kind of story for a society still rife with racial unrest, where men and boys of color deserve to be heroes rather than criminals or victims of police violence. A slim volume like this one cannot hope to exhaust all the possibilities of such a provocative topic. What it can do is show how *The Spider-Verse* blends animation styles, cultural reference points, and narrative self-awareness in ways that make it a milestone for racial representation in Hollywood – and arguably a contemporary classic of American youth culture.

Origins of a New Super-Teen

In August 1962, the 15th issue of Marvel's *Amazing Fantasy* series introduced a new superhero to its readers. On the cover, the hero casually detains a crook under his arm, swinging through urban airspace in a suit that has since remained largely unchanged – skin-tight with webbed patterning on red and blue; arachnoid icon across the breast; a mask with curiously opaque eyeholes. In this first view of the hero, two yellow dialogue bubbles offer hints about the character's identity: 'Though the world may mock Peter Parker, the timid teenager...' they read, '... it will soon marvel at the sight of Spider-Man'. Fast forward five decades, and Spider-Man is the crown prince of Marvel's current cultural dominance, with adventures that span three distinct Hollywood blockbuster franchises – not to mention the comics, television shows, novelizations, action figures, Halloween costumes, and countless other commercial tie-ins that have made Peter Parker the most visibly (and profitably) awkward teenager on the planet.

From that very first cover, Spider-Man's mystique and relatability come from a combination of amazing skill and youthful inexperience. Peter Parker's status as an everyday high schooler hiding his identity amidst routine adolescent problems instantly made him more relatable to audiences who could not identify as readily with adult heroes, who were usually more accomplished – jet-setting weapons dealers (Iron Man), pre-natural aliens (Superman), or independently wealthy vigilantes (Batman) – and could variously combine the conventions that Peter Coogan maps out in his oft-cited account of the genre's origins: mission, powers, identity, costume (Coogan 2006). In their 2012 co-edited volume celebrating Spider-Man's appeal after fifty years, Robert G. Weiner and Robert Moses Peaslee emphasize the importance of Spider-Man's status as both a 'young and a solo hero' (2012: 5). There had been other teenagers in comics prior to Peter Parker – Batman's Robin/Dick Grayson and Captain America's Bucky Barnes, to name a few – but they had primarily been sidekicks. Marvel executives were reportedly skeptical of a solo teen hero, which is why they consigned Spider-Man to the last number of their scuffling *Amazing Fantasy* series, and reportedly almost cancelled the issue just prior to its release, an anecdote of near failure that now only reinforces the character's underdog origin story. Since then, Spider-Man's debut has become one of the most celebrated single comic book issues in history, and the most famous collaboration of Marvel's super duo of writer Stan Lee and illustrator Steve Ditko.[4]

The need to gain experience, to stop being a kid, and the desire to be taken more seriously by his peers have always been core attributes of Spider-Man – as has the need to develop a stronger moral compass. In *Amazing Fantasy* 15, Peter is bitten by a spider at a lab demonstration, later discovering his powers and improvising a makeshift costume and web formula. Accustomed to being bullied by others, his first instinct is to show off his new talents at a disreputable wrestling competition, where he is discovered by a television producer who vows to make the

'Masked Marvel' a celebrity. Flashforward several months and Peter is Spider-Man, a celebrity performer. One night, while taking a break backstage, he sees a guard trying to catch a fleeing thief but declines to help apprehend him. Later, Peter returns home to find that his Uncle Ben has tragically been shot and killed. When he chases the assailant, he recognizes him as the same man he let escape earlier. The first episode famously ends with a regretful final panel, as Peter contemplates his own involvement in ensuring his uncle's death. A frame insert offers what would become the lasting moral dictum for future adventures: 'With great power there must also come – great responsibility'.

By now one of the most recognizable phrases in all of superhero lore, these words – here attributed to an omniscient narrator – would in some later versions come directly from the mouth of Uncle Ben. They are also the crux of a historically successful pairing of a superhero story with the conventions of a coming-of-age narrative (*bildungsroman*) and the conventional stock-and-trade of heroic pulp fiction. Later versions of Parker do get older – he graduates from high school, goes to college, and later gets a job as a photographer at *The Daily Bugle*, where he famously works for Spider-Man skeptic J. Jonah Jameson. But Parker's overall need for maturation remains a key part of his character in almost every version of the story, no matter his chronological age. In the decades since, numerous reformulations of Parker's adolescent adventures have become a constant reminder of a character who will always have *more* growing to do. Herein lies the essential vulnerability and appealing exuberance of a youth culture hero perpetually caught in a state of being *not quite ready* to be a superhero. The origin story recounted in that first comic has since been written and rewritten hundreds or even thousands of times.

Peter's combination of youthful inexperience and masked anonymity has also made Spider-Man quite portable. Initially, the character's movement occurred primarily in an *inter*-textual way – generating a slew of new episodes across and among different media – comics, books, theatrical adaptations, video games, live-action films, and of course his iconic first animated appearance in ABC's *Spider-Man*, which ran for three seasons (1967–70) and forever aligned the character with a theme song at least as infectious as any mutant arachnid bite could ever be ('Spider-Man, Spider-Man / Does whatever a spider can…'). Due to his enduring popularity, Spider-Man has also experienced one of the more unique journeys as a commodity in the contemporary culture industries. Unlike some of Marvel's other well-known characters, seemingly every stage of the character's pilgrimage across genres and media has been fraught with creative licensing squabbles. In the nascent field of media industry studies, that history of transactions has become a frequent touchstone for scholars, especially those interested in the emergent category of franchise filmmaking as both a corporate and creative category.[5]

At the turn of the last century, there was some question whether Spider-Man would ever see the silver screen like other superheroes. Ever since DC's breakout success with *Superman* (Richard Donner, 1978), Marvel had been poking around for opportunities to bring its most prized character to the screen. With this in mind, along with other film properties, the company founded Marvel Films in 1993 (Wong and Malone 2022). The problem, at that point, was that Marvel as a company was entirely based on making 'paper and plastic' and did not have the wherewithal to produce feature films (Wong and Malone 2022). In the early internet, pre-streaming context of the 1990s, the superhero genre had just begun to prove itself as a box office stalwart, most notably with the success of *Batman* (Tim Burton, 1989) and its sequels. Marvel Films accelerated its attempts to make Spider-Man cinema during that period, but it was unsuccessful due to a series of ill-fated production partnerships, first with Cannon Films, which went belly up in 1989 despite success with the Sylvester Stallone vehicle *Cobra* (George P. Cosmatos, 1986), and next with Carolco Pictures, which went bankrupt in 1996 without ever producing a promising Spider-Man script from *Terminator* director James Cameron, reportedly set to star Leonardo DiCaprio in the titular role.[6] Finally, after over a decade of false starts, Marvel reached a production arrangement in 2000 with Sony Pictures Entertainment (SPE), owner of Columbia Pictures and Sony Pictures Animation. In retrospect, the agreement looks like a rather bad decision, as it granted SPE and its Columbia subsidiary the exclusive rights to live-action Spider-Man film production, with Sony Pictures assuming the role of the distributor. Meanwhile, Marvel retained access to all other Spider-Man media moving into the 21st century (Wong and Malone 2022).

The Sony deal spurred an initial trilogy of successful big budget films – *Spider-Man* (2002), *Spider-Man* 2 (2004), and *Spider-Man* 3 (2007) – all directed by Sam Raimi and starring DiCaprio's good friend, Tobey Maguire. The first two Raimi films were received with great critical and box office success, ushering a new era of superhero cinema to the screen. However, the third instalment disappointed, leading to an eventual Sony-Raimi break-up before the production of his fourth film launched (Avala 2022). Undeterred, Sony sought to reboot the franchise again in the 2010s, producing two new titles – *The Amazing Spider-Man* (2012) and *The Amazing Spider-Man* 2 (2014) – both directed by Marc

Webb and starring Andrew Garfield. Despite their Marvel affiliation, the two Garfield films were still limited by the initial Sony deal, hence creatively and financially walled off from the other Marvel Comics properties, which were concurrently gaining steam as the Marvel Cinematic Universe (MCU), and had already acquired rights to Iron Man, Thor, Hulk, and the other core Avengers, housed at Disney since 2009 and produced by Kevin Feige – himself a veteran of the Raimi films from earlier in the decade.

Unfortunately, the second Webb/Garfield film's relative lack of success led to more creative and financial unrest during the making of the third instalment in that second franchise, and those worries were compounded by a high-profile data hack that released privileged information to the public in 2014 (Boot 2017). After the perceived failure of *The Amazing Spider-Man 2*, and the embarrassment of the leaked information, a beleaguered Sony Studios entered a sharing agreement with Disney's Marvel Cinematic Universe in 2015, which after months of negotiations, official and unofficial, was apparently finalized over an 'intimate lunch' between Sony producer Amy Pascal, Sony Pictures CEO Michael Lymon, and Marvel Entertainment CEO Ike Perlmutter (O' Connell 2022: 166). Under the new terms, Sony would retain the vast majority of the films' profits in exchange for granting Disney – and therefore Feige's MCU team – the right to use the character and take the 'creative lead' on all future movies (Goodman 2019).

The cooperation between Sony and Marvel also paved the way for a spread of Spider-Man characters across different media properties in the mid-to-late 2010s. While Tom Holland's incarnation of the character was set to appear in *Captain America: Civil War* (Joe and Anthony Russo, 2016) – and later headline a third live-action franchise – Pascal and her Sony colleague Avi Arad were tasked with re-purposing the company's numerous other properties, including developing film franchises for some of the high profile villains (Venom, Morbius), but also the numerous alternative Spider-People that had populated Marvel comics imprints for decades. Apparently thanks to a friendly working relationship with Feige – dating to their earlier collaboration on Raimi's films – Pascal and Arad bartered a deal with Marvel and convinced their collaborators that Lord and Miller would be an ideal choice for conceiving yet another Spider-Man movie, this one animated, that could take advantage of the collective holdings of the two companies. Pascal's confidence in the duo stemmed in part from their successful piloting of other youth-oriented box office successes with Sony in the past, notably *Cloudy with a Chance of Meatballs, 21 Jump Street* (2012), and *The Lego Movie* (2014) (Robinson 2018). From the outset, Lord and Miller embraced the project due to its promise of an expanded Spider-Man canon – and the chance to develop a character like Miles Morales was the main reason for their passion ('The Secrets Behind Spider-Man...' 2019).

If *The Spider-Verse* sprang from the aftermath of a somewhat awkward sharing agreement between Sony and Marvel, the uncertainty about its goals and prospects was not without some creative benefits. As the baby of Sony Animation, which was then a successful – if lesser-known – outfit on the landscape of American animation, the production process took a leisurely path over four years, largely out of the spotlight. The initial conception of the film dated back to at least 2014, as some of the emails leaked during the Sony hack show exchanges between Pascal and producer Doug Belgrad about how to bring a new concept to the screen based on Dan Slott's popular ongoing 'Spider-Verse' storyline in the comics, which featured multiple, intertwined characters and worlds ('Spider-Man Animated Movie...' 2015). A meeting between Pascal, Avad, Lord, and Miller then occurred sometime later in the year, and the first version of the screenplay – written by Lord and based on a romance between Miles and Gwen Stacy – was completed about a year after that (Robinson 2018). By the time Rodney Rothman joined the team in 2016, it was largely to help rethink that story arc, at which point he and Lord reconceived the film's entire premise according to a more pluralistic narrative style by using an ongoing brainstorming session that they called a 'story wheel', written on two whiteboards, and shared by Lord on social media in 2020 (Labonte 2020).

Meanwhile, the animation team, housed primarily at Sony Pictures Imageworks in Vancouver, embarked on a similarly developmental process, altering their work periodically as they received updates about the 'story wheel', and rapidly expanding the number of animators who worked on the film as the project grew in ambition. All in all, it took nearly a year to complete the initial, 10-second 'first look' sample of the animation style that was offered to the eager audiences of Comic Con in July 2017. Likewise, the theatrical teaser released in December of that same year had scant information about the story, featuring only two intertitles to convey a simple take-away message – this would be a film 'where more than one wears the mask'. Though it mostly showed various decontextualized views of the Brooklyn cityscape, the trailer did offer an extended look at Miles, his red-and-black suit, and his iconic 'leap of faith' that would feature on some of the promotional posters a year later. Probably playing to comic enthusiasts, the end of the teaser also shows Miles pulling back his mask, a gesture that resembles how he appeared on one version of the cover for his comics debut (see Figure 0.1).

Figure 0.1 Miles Morales unmasks in the teaser trailer

If the teaser trailer offers minimal information, it is not because of secrecy, but instead because the multiplicity of the story and visual design were far from ready to show the audience. After the film's release, it was reported that the production went from sixty animators in early 2017 to 142 that summer and a Sony-record 177 later in the year as the studio rushed to finish the film on time for a Christmas release in 2018 (Snyder 2019). Rewrites also continued on the script nearly right up to the release of the film in December 2018. It is not surprising then that most of the creators of *The Spider-Verse* describe the creative process as both 'collaborative' and 'stressful' leading up to its release – a product of the constant come-and-go between personnel in Los Angeles and Vancouver, who shared in an evolving, pluralistic, and sometimes disorganized emerging vision of what a new Spider-Man movie could be.

Diversity Done Right?

The arrival of a new, multiracial Spider-Man should also be seen in the context of a concerted effort by Marvel to democratize its forms of representation in the 2010s. At the heart of that effort initially was writer and illustrator Brian Michael Bendis, who felt a pressing need to promote more diversity in comic books, especially in the wake of the election of Barack Obama in 2008, and in light of his own adoption of two Black children. Though Bendis oversaw several other expansions of Marvel characters, including RiRi Williams/Ironheart (a Black female successor to Tony Stark/Iron Man) and Ms. Marvel/Kamala Khan (a teen Pakistani successor to Carol Danvers/Captain Marvel), the most successful of these efforts was Miles Morales, who first appeared in *Ultimate Fallout* #4, thrust into the role of the masked webslinger after Parker's untimely death. After several best-selling storylines cemented the character's popularity, brought to life by illustrator Sara Pichelli, Miles was then 'promoted' from his initial alternate universe (Earth-1610) to Marvel's primary universe (Earth-616) in 2014. Some sixty years after Peter Parker became the breakout (white) teen superhero to rescue Marvel against a cultural backdrop of Civil Rights activism, an Afro-Latino Spider-Man finally arrived to confront systemic inequities to which his predecessor was largely oblivious.

Marvel decision-makers would certainly have known that the climate was right for a multi-racial Spider-Man even before creating Miles. *Ultimate Fallout* #4 first appeared in 2011, but the Bendis-Pichelli collaboration was preceded by an upswell of energy on social media, largely spurred by the Twitter activism of actor-musician Donald Glover, then a regular cast member on the popular sitcom *Community* (NBC, 2009–15). Mobilizing his followers, Glover lobbied to be cast as Peter Parker for *The Amazing Spider-Man*, even posing at one point on his Twitter account wearing a Spider-Man costume. Although the role eventually went to a different (white) actor, Andrew Garfield, the impact of Glover's campaign drew the attention of Marvel executives, inspiring them to pursue the possibility of a Black Spider-Man in the comics, and eventually resulting in a small live-action cameo role for Glover in *Spider-Man: Homecoming* where he played Aaron Davis in a brief scene with Iron Man (Robert Downey Jr.).[7]

In hindsight, the release of *The Spider-Verse* in 2018 also makes it look like a harbinger for a larger trend. Though they had existed for decades in comics, techniques of pluralistic worldbuilding and multi-dimensionality reached mainstream live action filmmaking to stay in the 2020s. The Marvel list alone also includes some earlier and concurrent experiments with what Derek Johnson calls 'managing multiplicity' (2017) with the *X-Men* franchise, for which the studio culled numerous imprints from its troves, even reworking a 1981 storyline as a strategy for guiding a planned generational 'soft reboot' blending younger and older versions of the cast in *X-Men: Days of Future Past* (Bryan Singer, 2014). Of course, the narrative strategies of the subsequent decade make Marvel's earlier concern with redundancy look almost quaint, especially considering *The Spider-Verse*'s closest live-action cousin, *Spider-Man: No Way Home* (Jon Watts, 2021), a brainchild of many of the same executives at Sony and Marvel, who collaborated to produce Tom Holland's third appearance in the franchise.

Like the first two films in the trilogy, *No Way Home* is explicitly invested in motifs from the teen genre. More than its predecessors, it uses the conception of plural dimensions to reflect on previous itera-tions – bringing back numerous actors from the two previous *Spider-Man* franchises, including leads Tobey Maguire and Andrew Garfield, who reprise their roles as the earlier Peter Parkers. The MCU continued to assert multidimensional tropes in a series of outings of the early 2020s, including Raimi's directorial return for *Dr. Strange in the Multiverse of Madness* (2021) and the pluralistic adventure of *Shang-Chi and the Legend of the Ten Rings* (Destin Daniel Cretton, 2021). This is not even to mention other titles like *Ant-Man* (Peyton Reed, 2015), with its navi-gation of the Quantum Realm, or the celebrated diptych of *Avengers: Infinity War* (Anthony and Joe Russo, 2018) and *Endgame* (Anthony and Joe Russo, 2019), where the heroes must out-maneuver a supervillain, Thanos, moving across dimensional planes to collect the Infinity Stones and at one point even pausing to banter about the logic of alternate uni-verses in popular cinema.

At the time of writing, DC also seems bent on riding the multiverse wave, bringing back Michael Keaton, lead actor from *Batman* (1989), to star alongside Ben Affleck as mentors for Ezra Miller's dimension-hopping Barry Allen in *The Flash* (Andrés Muschietti, 2023). Meanwhile, the streaming series variously invested in parallel or multiple worlds seem almost too numerous to count these days – from the pre-teen horror thrills of the 'upside down' in *Stranger Things* (Netflix, 2017–), to the aberrant subjective lives of theme park androids in *Westworld* (HBO, 2016–18), or to more recent sci-fi adventures with explicit multi-dimensional content like *Parallels* (Disney+, 2022–) and *The Peripheral* (Amazon Prime, 2022–). And yet despite the spread of these multiverse tendencies across so many platforms and genres, none of these examples embraces the very act of narrating the process of multiple dimensions – or entangles it in the hero's journey – quite like *The Spider-Verse* and its sequels.

One should not exaggerate the newness of these genres or their penchant for cultural commentary. To the contrary, as Mark J.P. Wolf documents, literary production and popular culture have for centuries made use of imaginary worlds as a flexible device, creating alternative frames of reference within a dominant narrative form, or what he calls the history of 'subcreation' (Wolf 2012: 20–5). In many cases, Wolf argues, the function of a 'secondary world' is to enable forms of commentary or critique of the primary one, as do the lands of Lilliput and Brobdingnag in *Gulliver's Travels* (Jonathan Swift, 1726) (Wolf 2012: 78–80). In the 20th century, secondary worlds thrived most readily in the twin genres of fantasy and science fiction, both of which figured prominently in the development of the superhero genre around the 1920s.

Moreover, the arrival of an animated film like *The Spider-Verse* in 2018 should also be seen as in step with concurrent moves in live-action superhero movies and streaming content, which have recently turned their dominant position in American popular culture toward questions of inclusion and diversity. The most notable titles to mention here are probably *Black Panther* (Ryan Coogler, 2017) and its sequel *Wakanda Forever* (Ryan Coogler, 2023), but numerous other recent Marvel films explore ethnic and gender identities to varying degrees, including: casting a woman in a previously male role in *Captain Marvel* (Anna Boden and Ryan Fleck, 2019); privileging Asian heroism and martial arts lore in *Shang-Chi and the Legend of the Ten Rings*; adopting a collective approach to diverse casting in *The Eternals* (Chloé Zhao, 2021); and an interrogation of *Captain America*'s racial politics in the spinoff streaming series *The Falcon and the Winter Soldier* (Disney+, 2021–). For the MCU's primary competitor, DC Studios, the most prominent examples in this trend remain *Wonder Woman* (Patty Jenkins, 2017), *Wonder Woman 1984* (Patty Jenkins, 2020), and a recent entry, *The Blue Beetle* (2023), which offers a multigenerational depiction of its hero's Latinx family.

Worth mentioning here as well are Disney's concurrent moves toward diversity-oriented animated genre films like *Coco* (Molina and Unkrich, 2017), *Moana* (Clements and Musker, 2018), *Soul* (Docter, 2020), *Encanto* (Howard and Bush, 2021), and *Turning Red* (Shi, 2022); well-regarded streaming series like *Watchmen* (Hulu, 2019), *Lovecraft Country* (HBO, 2020), and *The Underground Railroad* (Amazon Prime, 2021); and the ongoing work of live-action directors like Spike Lee (*BlacKkKlansman* [2018]), Ava Duvernay (*Selma* [2016]), and especially Jordan Peele, whose massive popularity stems from the savvy, racialized re-working of genre tropes in a trio of blockbusters: *Get Out* (2016), *Us* (2018), and *Nope* (2022). Among these related titles, the most proximate to *The Spider-Verse* may be the live-action streaming series *Ms. Marvel* (Disney+, 2021), which performs a similar embrace of multimedia culture in telling the story of Kamala Khan, the New Jersey teen whose self-deprecating approach to her new superpowers allows for the earnest exploration of her family's Pakistani and Muslim cultural roots. While all these other examples do admirable work regarding how mainstream genres explore issues of racial representation and youth culture, it is doubtful that any of them do more generational heavy lifting than *The Spider-Verse*, which also advances its revision of Spider-Man as a self-consciously political act in favor of racial representation.

Into the Hypertext

By the end of *The Spider-Verse*, Miles emerges as an Afro-Latino youth superhero, one whose adventures can be embraced as *both* authentic and universal, proving his famous closing dictum that 'anyone can wear the mask'. To walk this fine line of identarian representation, the film deploys a pluralistic style that only begins with its innovative approach to 3D animation. Though these features do resemble other films of the post-modern era, the suggestion here will be that *The Spider-Verse* stands out from the crowd due to the audacity and persistence with which it pursues them. By creating and celebrating its own version of a fictional multiverse – a 'Spider-Verse' – in which invented characters and overlain animation styles interrelate with one another, the film creates a framework of hypothetical possibility that renders the premise of an Afro-Latino Spider-Man just one of many possible creative options. At the same time, the film uses other structural features to visually and emotionally center Miles Morales and his experiences. In other words, by the end of the film, Miles is *the* Spider-Man, and not just a racialized Spider-Man alternative among others.

To describe the various layers of how the film accomplishes this approach, this book embraces an ever-present and yet oft-overlooked descriptor in recent theories of transmedia and adaptation: hypertext.[8] The term is appealing in at least two senses. First, the prefix 'hyper' is an intuitive way to describe how the visual elements of *The Spider-Verse* land for most viewers in the first instance. Even compared with other recent Hollywood offerings, this is a film that offers an unusually energetic viewing experience, and calling it a 'hyper' style seems to fit – much in the way one might describe an unusually energetic child as 'hyperactive'. However, the constant mobility of the visual and sonic features of *The Spider-Verse* would not be as notable if they did not also relate to how the film creates its own complex web of inter-relationships that exist between the story arc of Miles Morales and its visual representation. In other words, the 'busy' qualities of this film's visual track are not mere window dressing, but a way to interconnect Miles' story with numerous other Spider-Man textualities and textures of the past, present, and future. It is as if we are watching this multi-plicity of possible representations unfold in real time, layered on top of one another, ready to spring to the fore.

Here one can also encounter the second sense of the full word, this one more explicitly theoretical. Though hypertext has long been pre-sent in the vocabulary of media theory and worldbuilding, it often gets overlooked in favor of other words that evoke stories and characters that move across platforms (*transtextual*) or in-between forms of production (*intertextual*). For literary theory, all these textual prefixes derive from a set of terms initially proposed by French narrative theorist Gérard Genette, who coined them in an influential work on literary tropes called *Palimpsests: Literature in the Second Degree* (1982), translated to English in 1997, which became a bedrock for later studies of 'intertextuality' across cultural fields. Less exploited by theorists – yet equally present in his account – is the term *hypertext*, described as 'a text's relationship to all of the texts that came before it' (1997: 5). For Genette, hypertextual relationships are those that draw on a present work's connections to the body of collected prior knowledge of itself – a dimension that he calls the *hypotext* (ibid.). A structural dimension of a text's lifespan, the hypertext draws on an almost archetypical sense of temporality, and of a consciousness of those texts that came before, whether readers are aware of their presence or not. And whereas all cultural production potentially draws to some degree on the flux of energy between *hyper* and *hypo* relationships, not all of them work to represent the dynamics between them in an explicit way.

For the purposes of this volume, what makes *The Spider-Verse* a hypertextual film is that the act of discerning numerous relationships to previous Spider-Man stories and characters (the film's *hypotext*) becomes both a concern of the plot and an active part of the viewing experience. For instance, even before the story begins for Miles, *The Spider-Verse* hints at the complexity of its system of references with a disruptive opening pre-credit sequence, blended into a mix of crackling lap dissolves and audible glitches on the soundtrack. First on the screen, the white lettering of the Sony logo gradually grows on a stark black background. As the letters advance smoothly into the foreground, they suggest three-dimensional space as they 'pass' the borders of the frame. Eventually, the 'O' of the word disperses 'beyond' our visual field, changing form as it gets closer and closer until it looks like a series of patterned dots. The immersive visual shift that occurs in these moments is the first glimpse of the film's cinematic rendition of 'half-toning' – a technique common to comic books of the 1980s and 1990s – wherein geometrically arranged 'Ben-Day' dots in various sizes create shades and textures on the printed page ('How "Spider-Man ..."' 2019). Next, the iconic Columbia Pictures logo appears, not with its usual cadence, but instead in a series of lap dissolves that reveals numerous previous versions of the logo. Arriving one after another, even on top of each other, the logos exhibit stylistic diversity: a flickering black-and-white negative image; a color version; a dark screen peppered with what appears to be neon outlines of flickering clothing.

Perhaps most memorably, the central, torch-bearing, female figure is even temporarily supplanted at one point by a moving, animated cowgirl who steps forward, shooting left and right. Cartoonish sounds of gunfire ring out just as the words 'A Sony Company' appear beneath her feet (see Figure 0.2). Potential questions abound. Who is this cowgirl? How is she related to Columbia? What is her relevance to *The Spider-Verse*? And who, come to think of it, is that draped, torch-bearing woman that she supplants for a few seconds? As if on cue, numerous visible glitches jostle the screen as the image track itself appears to skip several frames, and then the Marvel Studios logo arrives, bathed in what appears to be a red filter as comic book pages 'flip' in a familiar manner – recognizable from other recent live-action franchises. Just as the words 'In association with' flicker above the pages, the Marvel lettering appears, itself subject to the shudder of constant reframing and dissolves that display different versions and fonts of the lettering, along with what appears to be blotchy spray-paint.

By the time the words 'Sony Animation Studios' first arrive on screen, the audience has thus already traversed numerous audible jumps and surface textures, as if to suggest the immanent coexistence of multiple versions. From the first instance, then, *The Spider-Verse* plays on the distinctions between what adaptation theorist Linda Hutcheon refers to as 'knowing' and 'unknowing' audiences (Hutcheon 2012: 120–128). For most viewers, lacking in-depth knowledge of Columbia logos and cartoons, these moments could be experienced merely as brief, playful interruptions – in line with the approach of Hollywood credits sequences for generations. Those with previous knowledge (or who bother to research) will note at least a half dozen

Figure 0.2 Who is this cowgirl?

torch-bearing figures flitting by on the screen here, from a 1930s–40s version in black-and-white, all the way to the more recognizable 1993 revamp by illustrator Michael Deas, based on photographs of model Jenny Joseph by photographer Karen Lawrence (Muzdakas 2022). Meanwhile, the cowgirl draws on even more obscure origins, replicating the opening credits of an oft-forgotten Columbia-produced Jane Fonda revenge Western called *Cat Ballou* (Elliot Silverstein, 1965).[9] Finally, in a sort of winking flourish, the credit sequence ends with a white stamp on a stark, black background that reads 'Approved by the Comics Code Authority'. Likely mysterious to a majority of young viewers, the reference resounds differently for older comic collectors in the audience – many of whom will recognize the label from their oldest comics, which sported the stamp to refer to a 'loosely governed' institution that 'kept harmful or offensive material out of storylines' in the early industry (O'Connell 2022: 219).

This successive troubling of the company logos constitutes the film's first gesture toward a multiplicity of possible reference points. Of course, any or all these details can be readily glossed over. Even those viewers who are attentively in their seats to watch could allow them to flit by unnoticed, dismissing them as the usual embellishments of a 'pop' influenced credit sequence. And even without the deep-dive details afforded by a quick internet search, most audiences could still gather meaning from this more general gesture. This is a film with a complicated multi-media parentage, one that resembles the journey of Spider-Man as a character, and the multifaceted process of creation that lies behind the conception of the film. Audiences are, after all, about to enter *The Spider-Verse* – which many viewers will already know from trailers and teasers is a film that embraces generic multiplicity achieved on a 'meta' level. Yet these first few moments of screen time also signal what will come, not only by suggesting the rich, fluctuating history of traces that lies behind the present images, but also by showing how multiple generic conventions can come to cohabit the frames of a single image. This technique will become the film's stock and trade as the plot moves on.

Toward Continuing Analysis

The goal of a slim volume like this one cannot be to trace the complexity of every reference in a film like *The Spider-Verse*. Though it will touch where appropriate on the complicated backstory of the Spider-Man franchise, it also does not pretend to offer an encyclopedic reference tool for cataloguing characters or plot points in the film, many of which have numerous antecedents on the page and screen. For those who are interested in those angles, online critics and fan communities have already collaborated to do a rather comprehensive job (Gvozden 2018). Instead, the guiding principle in this book will be to consider how the visual and sonic multiplicity of this film relates to its larger thematic goals as a superhero youth film invested in diverse representation. Peter Parker's opening catchphrase in the film – 'let's do this one last time' – is purposefully ironic but also pliable, opening space for other forms of commentary and reflection. Within seconds of that invitation, the audience knows that the film in progress proposes neither *one* authoritative version of events nor any *last* accounting of them, but rather an opening for an entirely new version of known events to unfold.

Preserving this spirit of plurality and possibility, each of the sections of this book aims to show how *The Spider-Verse* uses a hypertextual design strategy on its surface to craft a space for Miles Morales to assert his multiracial identity as a new icon of Afro-Latino boyhood. Putting a recent history of media and adaptation theory in conversation with scenic and stylistic examples, Chapter 1 shows how the film deploys a referential style that is both multiple and falsifiable, creating a flurry of internalized 'Easter Eggs' that reach beyond the film, but also anticipate and condition numerous possible forms of viewer engagement with the story of Miles Morales. Chapter 2 follows this demonstration by showing how the film's creative team honored the film's comic roots by deploying an innovative, hypertextual approach to CGI. Using the stylistic traits of at least three visual artforms – cinema, comics, and animated cartoons – the animators offer a visual grammar that references multiple forms of technology at one time, resulting in a textured viewing experience that sheds light on the 'past lives' of Spider-Man, while dramatizing various consequences of how any representation draws on a deep archive of past versions (*hypotext*).

Building on these theoretical and structural analyses of technique, the book then moves to more slippery questions of cultural interpretation – suggesting ways in which critics and audiences have thus far made use of the hypertextual features outlined earlier. Chapter 3 pushes beyond the surface of animation, showing additional ways that the film incorporates references to other forms of cultural production to racialize the conventions of the familiar Spider-Man origin story. Drawing on a deep reservoir of reference points – from *Great Expectations* to Air Jordans – *The Spider-Verse* creates a visual and sonic vocabulary that subtly anticipates the specter of systemic racism, endorsing a type of critical thinking about racial awareness as an epistemological shift to anti-racism. Finally, in the Conclusion section, the book explores how energies from *The Spider-Verse* continue to spill beyond one film's borders, making Miles Morales an icon of youth culture for Marvel and Sony across media. The book finishes, fittingly, with the brief post-credit scene in the film, which recreates a viral Spider-Man 'pointing' meme that both preceded the film's pre-production phase and inspired the plot arc of its sequel. The end of this treatment of *Into the Spider-Verse* therefore invites fans and critics to continue replicating the games of anticipation and re-interpretation encouraged by the film itself. As if to ratify the centrality of this re-reading process, the producers made it the main selling point for *Across the Spider-Verse* – released in the summer of 2023. Inspired by Miles and his courage, this book therefore enacts its own similar 'leap of faith' – hoping to account for the engaging style and savvy racial politics of a poignant animated feature film.

Notes

1 Box office numbers from *Spider-Man: Into the Spider-Verse*, were obtained from *Box Office Mojo* (https://www.boxofficemojo.com/releasegroup/gr4195373573/).
2 *The Spider-Verse* is currently the highest ranked superhero film listed on Rotten Tomatoes with a 97% 'Fresh' aggregate score (https://editorial.rot tentomatoes.com/guide/best-superhero-movies-of-all-time/). It came in at #6 on a Top-50 list compiled by *Rolling Stone* (Fear et al. 2022).
3 The eventual international total for the sequel approached $700 million. See the entry for '*Spider-Man: Across the Spider-Verse*' on *Box Office Mojo* (https://www.boxofficemojo.com/release/rl2812183041/).
4 While Stan Lee and Steve Ditko are usually credited with the character, fellow comic art legend Jack Kirby and his partner Joe Simon also claimed on multiple occasions that the character was first conceived in the 1950s. Whatever the case, the emergence of Spider-Man represents a moment when comic books realized that they could capitalize on the youth market by making a teenager a primary hero rather than a sidekick (see Weiner and Peaslee [2012: 6]).
5 Derek Johnson has written widely about the combination of strategic and creative elements that made superhero films the ideal property for Hollywood of the 2010s. See in particular Johnson (2012), Johnson (2013) and Johnson (2017).
6 Best known for low-budget action films like *American Ninja* (Sam Firstenberg, 1985) and its sequels, Cannon was actively seeking larger properties – and had found recent success with *Cobra*. Unfortunately, the company went bankrupt in 1989, unable to fulfil its hopes for Spider-Man, so Marvel once again regathered its screen rights and looked for another production partner. Marvel's next flirtation was with Carolco Pictures, through whom Marvel first entertained what would become a series of unsuccessful negotiations with MGM – hindered, among other things, by a complex set of

legal disputes over unproduced scripts by *Terminator* director James Cameron and the rights to make *James Bond* films. Marvel was ultimately, once again, without a partner to make Spider-Man a live-action, big screen commodity.

7   Speculation about Glover's future involvement in Marvel properties continues to this day – a phenomenon recently abetted by a second brief intertextual cameo as Aaron in Miguel O'Hara's Spider Society during a scene of *Spider-Man: Across the Spider-Verse* (2023). This time, Aaron is shown actually wearing his costume as The Prowler, imprisoned as one of the many 'anomalies' that threaten the structure of the multiverse.

8   See Hutcheon (2012) and Meikle (2019) for representative examples of how the term has been used (and not used) in the adaptation field. A related but different use of the term 'hypertext' has also accumulated a parallel literature more related to the operational experiences brought about by the advent of computer technology and the network archiving of data – as in the term 'hyperlink'. Though it is beyond the scope of the current volume, this genealogy of thought arguably begins with Vannuvar Bush's prophetic early article 'As We May Think' (first published in *The Atlantic* in July 1945) and extends forward to more contemporary cultural critics like Castells (1996) who theorize networked culture.

9   A deep dive into the history of the Columbia woman and her inspiration – which goes back to American nationalist propaganda and its roots in the Roman goddess Minerva – or into Jane Fonda's career is beyond the scope of this chapter. For more information, see Beck (2018).

1 Into a Spider-Verse of References

'I'm pretty sure you know the rest'

Minutes into *The Spider-Verse* a voice-over narration addresses the audience: 'Alright, let's do this one last time. My name is Peter Parker. I was bitten by a radioactive spider and for ten years, I've been the one – and *only* – Spider-Man. I'm pretty sure you know the rest'. Voiced here by Chris Pine, Parker sounds earnest but also skeptical that his claim – and by extension this film – will amount to anything novel for the viewer. As if to substantiate that doubt, a barrage of visual and sonic references to the Spider-Man media sphere follows his words, summing up the major plot points of nearly every Spider-Man story ever told. Peter's eponymous Uncle Ben appears, uttering the words 'With great power comes great responsibility', before disappearing into a shiny void. A series of animated re-enactments of scenes from the Sam Raimi/Tobey Maguire trilogy of *Spider-Man* films (2002, 2004, 2006) ensue: 'I saved a bunch of people' (Spider-Man stops a moving subway train with his web); 'I saved the city' (he rescues innocent restauranteurs from an exploding window); 'I saved the city again … and again and again' (still more scenes unfurl on a horizontally split screen resembling comic book panels). Next a montage, a series of different commercialized products: 'I have a cereal' (a young girl pours out some Spider-Man breakfast cereal); 'Did a Christmas album' (Spider-Man sings along to carols in a Santa Claus hat); 'I have an excellent theme song' (a blurry television screen along with the opening notes of 'Spider-Man, Spider-Man...'); 'and, um, I have a so-so popsicle' (a smaller frame shows a melted red-and-white popsicle resembling his mask).

A salient first impression of this movie is its nimble surface energy. Geared to cue memories of both comic books and previous *Spider-Man* movie franchises, the details of this opening sequence might land as sardonically celebratory, impossibly numerous, or both. Parker's summaries are quick and seem almost dismissive – he is pretty sure the

DOI: 10.4324/9781003166962-2

audience will know them anyway. However, upon closer inspection, each of the mini episodes he narrates here also reckons critically in some way with its source material. One recognizable callback to *Spider-Man* (2002) pairs with the phrase 'I fell in love'. It appears, at first glance, to be a redux of the memorable kiss between that film's Spider-Man (Tobey Maguire) and Mary Jane Watson (Kirsten Dunst). Featured prominently in trailers and on posters of that first live-action *Spider-Man* movie, the kiss between a partially masked hero and his lady love remains one of the more indelible images from the Raimi trilogy, encapsulating the romance between the two characters, as well as their entanglement in Peter's hidden superhero identity. Upon brief inspection, however, one notes that the version we see in *The Spider-Verse* does not check out; it is instead a clear reversal of the physical positions of the two characters from the original image (see Figure 1.1).

As just one of a flurry of nods to Spider-Man in various guises, this fleeting moment of screen time offers an example of the kinds of citational complexity that occur moment-to-moment in *The Spider-Verse*. The kissing scene is not mere mimicry, as it is Mary Jane (and not Peter) who is suspended in the air, in a reversal of the Raimi version that makes no logical sense in the context of a story where he (and not she) is the webslinger. Not only that, but the version offered in *The Spider-Verse* also *anticipates* that viewers will notice these differences. Subsequently the image 'pulls back' in an animated rendition of a dolly-out, revealing that Mary Jane is, in fact, the one suspended screen-left, from what appears to be a fire escape ladder. Were we to pursue the connotations of the image even further, other furtive references might come to light. For instance, the gendered role-reversal could constitute an oblique gesture to yet another iconic New York city alleyway encounter in *West Side Story* (Wise and Robbins, 1961).

Figure 1.1 Mary Jane and Peter kiss in *Spider-Man: Into the Spider-Verse*

Whatever flights of interpretation these moments might evoke, it is as if they are crafted with purposefully plural meanings – not only echoing famous micro-moments from Spider-Man movie lore but pointing out the inherent instability or even falsifiability of each one in turn. At some point, only the most assiduous fans will be able to track both the progression of this complex narrative and these numerous gestures toward actual and hypothetical versions in real time. Some, like super-fan and podcaster Dan Gvozden, have done so quite exhaustively.[1] But even viewers with a less encyclopedic knowledge of Spider-Man through history can appreciate this film's act of *inviting* – indeed even *teaching* – them a mode of repeated, internalized analysis. This incessant reflexivity, carried to the point of absurdity in some places, is what gives *The Spider-Verse* one of its more striking features, even when placed among the current proliferation of superhero films, and even amidst Hollywood's recent trend toward stories that make use of parallel or multiple universes. Further, it is this nervous energy that also allows the film to aptly characterize its youthful protagonist, whose age-appropriate search for racial, cultural, and individual identity often motivates the swirl of formal flourishes around him. To better describe these dynamics, this chapter engages recent media theory and criticism in search of a vocabulary that can capture the structural features of a film perpetually engaged in a process of *becoming* itself – all while amplifying the story of a teen character who is doing the exact same thing.

Multiple Multiverses

Even the cursory description of the montage described above cannot avoid encountering a slew of deliberate hiccups – awkward sidesteps, winking mistakes, overt mischaracterizations. The interpretive game proposed here is then not simply to gesture at other related films or to disperse a serialized story across multiple films as in the MCU. It is also not a mere feature-length version of Marvel's popular comic-turned-streaming *What If?* series – where each installment probes a hypothetical reversal or alternate scenario of canonic accounts of a superhero story. Rather, *The Spider-Verse* is a movie that is in many ways about a deliberate play between *actual* and *virtual* references, mixing clear reverence for some past entries (*Spider-Man 2* features prominently) with playful derision for others (Peter mocks the cringe-worthy dancing scene from *Spider-Man 3*), and spanning from the 'what already has been', to the 'what never was' or the 'absolutely ridiculous'.

These features make plain that the premise – indeed the very title – of this film entails entering a mode of active, critical viewership attuned to an ever-evolving palette of choices. Self-consciously evoking transmedia franchises of the superhero variety and otherwise, this is a movie that pulses with the creative dynamism and winking referentiality of contemporary American youth culture. Equipped with this awareness of its own instability and potential for disruption, the film propels forward with a splashy admixture of layered animation styles, hooks from a popular hip-hop soundtrack, and intermittent moments where the images themselves look to be ripped from comic book splash pages at one moment, then sprayed with paint-can street art the next. Though all these relationships may not be recognizable on a first or second pass, their sheer proliferation ensures a movie experience susceptible to continual rewatching and analysis online and elsewhere – or what Jason Mittell has called the 'forensic fandom' of the multiplatform era, wherein avid fans gather to generate endless, unfolding takes on well-known material, and where managing a multiplicity of inputs becomes a design feature rather than a bug (Mittell 2012).

An ability to write compellingly across these broad-based changes has helped Henry Jenkins' theorization of 'transmedia storytelling' sustain influence over the past two decades, offering scholars and critics a way to describe how multimedia franchises cull patterns of meaning across multiple platforms. In conversation with contemporaneous scholars whose work had also begun to carve space for a 'transmedia' theory – among them Janet Murray (1997) and Barbara Klinger (2006) – Jenkins first articulates his ideas with reference to the two sequels of *The Matrix* (Wachowskis [2001] and [2003]) (2006), and in other writing and on his prolific personal websites 'Confessions of an Aca-Fan' and 'Pop Junctions' (2007; 2009). In the most widely cited chapter of *Convergence Culture*, entitled 'Searching for the Origami Unicorn: *The Matrix* and Transmedia Storytelling', Jenkins posits what he calls an 'ideal' form of transmedia storytelling, which he claims 'unfolds across multiple media platforms with each new text making a distinctive and valuable contribution to the whole' (Jenkins 2006: 96). Crucially, each of the individual entries must be both 'self-contained' and a potential 'point of entry into the franchise as a whole' such that 'reading across the media sustains a depth of experience that motivates more consumption' (ibid.). Finally, each of the different media niches (films, television, games, comics, books) can work together to 'attract multiple constituencies' by 'pitching the content somewhat differently' (ibid.).

Over the past decade plus, the concept of 'transmedia storytelling' has progressed from theoretical trend to industrial buzzword and back again. In the meantime, the spread of social media and arrival of streaming giants like Netflix have stoked widespread adoption of multiplatform entertainment practices in the culture industries, offering numerous real-world examples that have both affirmed Jenkins' original concepts and shifted the ground beneath them. In his initial thoughts on *The Matrix* and its extensions (among them *The Animatrix* collection of short films, the *Enter the Matrix* video game, and the graphic novel series affiliated with the franchise), Jenkins describes the Wachowskis' goal of creating a film franchise where the experience of narrative could be 'distributed' across media in a way that does not privilege any one central text. In the process of describing these ambitions and their challenges – most notably the narrative incoherence of *The Matrix Reloaded* (2003) – Jenkins admits that *The Matrix* is likely a limit-case experiment, one that ultimately fails despite its honest ambitions (2006: 93–130). Indeed, numerous other examples of transmedia narrative extensions over the past two decades have shown that the economic reality of the media industries make the ideal 'balanced' form of transmedia exceedingly rare, as the majority of audience members cannot or will not engage with every extension of a franchise. As Jason Mittell observes in his lucid survey of these dynamics, most examples of transmedia storytelling actually adopt what he calls an 'unbalanced' form in practice, giving precedence to a centralized text – often a feature film or streaming series – and putting numerous others (video games, graphic novels, streaming series, etc.) in secondary positions around the so-called 'mothership' (2015: 292–318).

No example of these features has been more visible than the Marvel Cinematic Universe. Beginning with *Iron Man* (Jon Favreau, 2008), each entry in the 'MCU' – as it is usually called – has unfurled a new facet of what now resembles a tapestry of interconnected stories, an impressive run of thirty feature films (and counting) where each successive entry seems to attain a more historic scale of narrative interconnectedness and box office performance. In the 2020s, as Marvel's success expands, its Disney parentage has attempted a similar expansion with *Star Wars* and its many other commodities on Disney+, making the interlinkages between media texts less a novelty than a baseline expectation for leading forms of popular streaming platform production. Recently, film theorists have also begun to describe how contemporary media franchises have developed their own citational style. A recent study of franchise adaptations by Kyle Meikle, for instance, highlights the way recent franchise films of the 2010s tend to leverage audience knowledge of an 'intertextual network' that both precedes and exceeds the film they are watching (2019: 10). That network may resemble the 'ongoing whirl of intertextual references' that Robert Stam describes in his influential earlier essay on film adaptation (2000: 66), but it is also clear that films released in the digital era draw on what Meikle calls audience 'pre-awareness' in a more thoroughgoing way than their predecessors.

Other scholars have explored the specific ways that superhero films deploy particular forms of citationality. In an effort to specify how this works in the current incarnation of the MCU, Marie-Laure Ryan proposes the idea of 'transfictionality' as a strategy for understanding how characters cross over from one commodity to another while maintaining a coherent sense of storyworld (2013: 361). And in an essay that anticipates the plural dimensions of a film like *The Spider-Verse*, Felix Brinker argues that 'the franchise's story world is only one among many succeeding incarnations of the Marvel Universe and, accordingly, relates to multiple different earlier incarnations of its superhero protagonists in comic books, film, television, and elsewhere' and that the interconnections among them draw on older forms of seriality that have long been part of the logics of comic book storytelling (Brinker 2017: 212–3).

Brinker suggests that while some of these citational forms do presume linear connections across a coherent story world (the 'transmedial' fictions described by Jenkins and Ryan), others instead operate according to what he calls 'compounding or cumulative' forms – those most common in the remakes, reboots, or re-brandings of characters that had already been quite common in the serial tradition and comics of the past (220). In this sense, the way that the MCU articulates its characters plays on the previous knowledge of audience members, in many cases with obscure references that can be quite rarefied, requiring extensive knowledge of previous iterations to be identified (221). Brinker describes the particular use of seriality in the superhero blockbuster as 'hyper-referential' or 'a style of storytelling that invites viewers to continue their engagement elsewhere and to watch sequels and spin-offs, read many-decade-old source materials and newly released superhero comics, or peruse paratextual materials online' (2022: 5). A related analysis by James C. Taylor seeks to outline the formal construction of the Marvel films as their own novel addition to the contemporary cultural landscape, a series where 'meanings of previous texts are harnessed, reaffirmed and reworked' by films that form 'intertextual relations with other nodes in the textual network' (2021a: 151).

The opening sequence discussed above offers an effective preview of the film to come, presenting a world where the possibility for perplexing misrecognitions and plural interpretations ('Let's do this one last time…') becomes *itself* the entry point for viewers of any level of knowledge. Some of this dimension of *The Spider-Verse* is doubtless a difference of degree from numerous other examples Mark J.P. Wolf's historical account of transmedia forms is a helpful reminder here, as he shows how 'secondary worlds' are a much older phenomenon of cultural production, germinating throughout a Western (and to some extent Eastern) history of ideas leading up to more recent incarnations in popular culture, and particularly in the genres of science fiction and fantasy prevalent in comics (2012: 96–106). Moreover, Hollywood filmmaking has for generations dealt in games of self-reference and nostalgia. David Bordwell, for instance, suggests that the weight of Hollywood's intertextual heritage leads to a generation of current directors whose stylistic approaches reflect the pursuit of novelty despite a de facto knowledge of their own 'belatedness' in an industry where 'everything has already been done' (Bordwell 2006: 22–3). Meanwhile, adaptation scholars over the past several decades have for some years observed an intensification or acceleration of that game's reflexive interrelationships. Linda Hutcheon, for instance, describes the art of contemporary adaptation as a constant post-modern juggling act between how texts appeal to 'knowing' and 'unknowing' audiences who, nevertheless, both represent crucial segments of any film's commercial aspirations (Hutcheon 2012: 120–8).

And yet, as a case study for these ideas, *The Spider-Verse* also seems to push past these initial definitions – or at least to take them for granted to a degree far beyond most of its live action counterparts. Unlike the MCU, for instance, which increasingly looks like a tapestry woven between each new feature film or streaming series, rewarding audience knowledge of their interlinkages, this is a film where the connections between various texts, and indeed speculations and unauthorized expansions form the very basis of the story-world itself. As has already been noted, Parker's voiceover and the accompanying montage draw so overtly on an entire pre-history of Spider-texts that it is impossible to enter 'into' *The Spider-Verse* (as proposed by the title) without a sense of the 'always were' or the 'maybe has been'. Meanwhile, unlike *The Matrix* trilogy, which for Jenkins in many ways fails to reach the 'ideal' of transmedia that his theory proposes – especially in its over-dependence on its smaller extensions like the video game *Enter the Matrix* – *The Spider-Verse* seems to purposely blur the distinction between its own fictional references and the more authentic ones, and to make a state of partial knowledge of viewers the very basis for its narrative exploration of its characters.

In other words, this is a film that short-circuits critiques of its own authenticity by muddling the very possibility of 'authentic' references at the outset. Since some viewers probably do not know the references, the opening montage teaches them how to read them. This tension between a 'present' text and its antecedents has been a preoccupation of post-modern literary criticism. For his part, Jenkins acknowledges these debts by culling the concept of 'transmedia storytelling' out of Umberto Eco's post-modern conception of the 'cult film' (Eco 1985) and Pierre Lévy's notion of 'collective intelligence' (Lévy 1999). Transmedia stories, he wagers, satisfy audience cravings for 'gap filling' by proposing an incomplete world worthy of additive creation, an activity that audiences have always done collectively, but that internet platforms make both more frequent and more traceable to researchers. As Jenkins points out, most audiences probably do not have enough information to 'get' *The Matrix* and its sequels, but they do have the resources to build an online community to do so after the fact (Jenkins 2006: 116).

In her widely cited *A Theory of Adaptation*, Hutcheon draws on similar recent dynamics in proposing an approach that can adopt three critical perspectives on the same remixed materials we often see at the multiplex – as a product for consumption, a process of creation, and a process of reception. Much in the vein of Stuart Hall (1980) and other media scholars before her, Hutcheon conceives of a multidimensional way for meaning to circulate between makers and consumers of text. In her sense, the 'product' focuses on the poetic features of a work 'in itself', whereas the 'process of creation' emphasizes authorial, cultural and contextual inputs ('encoding'), and the 'process of reception' looks at what audiences and readers make of them ('decoding') (Hutcheon 2012: 113–33). No surprise, of course, that Hutcheon views these three aspects as layered parts of the same essential dynamic of criticism, echoing the French title of Genette's original book (1982) while describing her central metaphor of the *palimpsest*.

Originally a term for medieval scrolls whose reused surfaces retained subtle traces of previous stages of inscription and re-inscription, the palimpsest offers an early historical example of how traces of past derivations can haunt later iterations, even visible to viewers with knowledge of them, or sensitivity to their furtive presence. Moreover, these immanent layers – whether conscious or not to the individual – interact with one another in what Hutcheon calls the 'palimpsestuous intertextuality' of audience experience, wherein many recent adaptations are 'multilaminated' and are 'directly and openly connected to recognizable other works' making that connection 'part of their formal identity, but also what we might call their hermeneutic identity'

(Hutcheon 2012: 21). The 'multilaminated' feeling described by Hutcheon goes some way to pinpointing what seems to be at play in *The Spider-Verse*. Moreover, a 'palimpsestuous' dynamic is part of transmedia storytelling as conceived by Jenkins, which is often designed so as to leverage audience awareness of the same. He characterizes this as the 'drillable' nature of the stories, drawing on Eco's concept of the cult film, where part of the currency of moments in a film sprout from a certain textual imperfection – providing viewers with incomplete story worlds rather than organic wholes (Jenkins 2006; 2009). This imperfection or unexplained element then makes way for plausible extensions of the world later on.

What is rarer, however, is to see an individual text that seeks to depict the shakiness of a referential relationship between possible worlds in real time. It is here, I think, that another term is needed, one that captures not just the furtive copresence of past and present versions and readings (palimpsest) or the linkages to other possible media depictions (transmedia) but rather a constant, palpable sense of aesthetic incompleteness that arrives when a film predicates itself on the constant possibility of going elsewhere, or becoming another version of itself, at any moment whatsoever. *The Spider-Verse*'s film's trio of directors have moved well beyond the 'belatedness' of contemporary Hollywood cinema (Bordwell 2006: 22–3). Rather than cave to a constant feeling of creating media culture in an era when everything has 'already been done' before, they craft a film that bathes in a form of creativity that can celebrate redundancy – and the audience's own knowledge of it. To analyze the frenzy of visual and aesthetic reference points in play in *The Spider-Verse*, it is essential to have a vocabulary to better target a film that posits external reference points that are nevertheless *internal* to understanding how a particular text works.

It is here that I turn to another term – *hypertext* – a descriptor which, while already contained in many older accounts of textual poetics and adaptation, has often been subordinated to the abiding interest in the 'trans' or the 'inter' textual energies described by Jenkins and others. First conceived in the 1960s by programmers to imagine how the possible linkages between stored data on futuristic computers could eventually change society, something like a concept of 'hypertext' has also been deployed by theorists of media communication like Manuel Castells, who describes how media practices shift in the age of computers and networks (1996). By now, the term has echoes in a far more mundane connotation as well, connected to the norm of website design wherein written digital text can be highlighted to indicate a connection to other locations on the web (hyperlinks).

Furthermore, in terms of narratology, or the study of how different media tell stories, the term was adopted by French theorist Gérard Genette well before the age of the internet. In Genette's sense, hypertext is a way to account for a particular subset of the transtextual relationships that he observes in literary language, and specifically for how a present text contains innumerable relationships with its predecessors (1997: 5).[2] Genette deploys a typology of transtextual relations with respect to literary works, which he theorizes with five overlapping forms: *intertextuality* (the co-presence of two or more texts); *paratextuality* (other messages or commentaries that surround a text, either internal ones like epigraphs or external ones like book reviews); *metatextuality* (a text that comments on or critiques another text); *architextuality* (a text's often quite variable relationship to the genre of its title, especially when it is translated or adapted to another artform); and, finally, *hypertextuality* (a text's relationship to all of the texts that came before it, a body of collected prior knowledge that he calls the *hypotext*).

These Genettian terms have since become influential guideposts for numerous scholars in the field of adaptation studies, which repurposes them in various ways to chart the connections that can occur as works travel between different disciplines and artforms. Drawing equally on Genette and the work of Mikhail Bakhtin, Robert Stam proposes transtextuality as an artful way to pursue a more flexible relationship to stories that move between media, avoiding the hierarchical preference often given to those that came first (2000: 54–5). For Stam, this tendency has been particularly egregious regarding filmic adaptations, which are often judged by their fidelity to novelistic predecessors, hamstrung by the 'automatic difference' between film and literature (55). Armed with Genette's terms, critics can instead ask malleable questions about the dynamics of influence, moving beyond conversations about whether a movie is faithful to the 'letter' or 'spirit' of a work that came before. This, for Stam, makes the fifth form – hypertext – 'the most suggestive' of the bunch. He writes:

> Filmic adaptations, in this sense, are hypertextual elaborations of a single hypotext that have been transformed by operations of selection, amplification, concretization, and actualization. [...] Indeed, the diverse prior adaptations can form a larger, cumulative hypotext that is available to the filmmaker who comes relatively 'late' in the series.
>
> (Stam 2000: 66)

Though he does not spell them out as completely in his essay, Stam also has subjective dynamics in mind, namely those that are at play not only for a work's creator (the author or director or artist), but those of uptake as well – reading, viewing, playing – wherein two individuals will never have the exact same relationship to the numerous elements and references woven into the fabric.

The Spider-Verse, in its pre-emptive gesture to include all current audience members to some degree among a 'knowing' relationship to its reference points also challenges the most common usage of another Genettian media term – the *paratext*. While Genette is careful to point out that none of his proposed terms is exclusive or exhaustive, the recent proliferation of film franchises has encouraged scholarly focus on the relationships between 'primary' and 'secondary' texts that occupy or otherwise inflect a common act of worldbuilding. As elaborated on by Jonathan Gray in *Show Sold Separately: Promos, Spoilers and Other Media Paratexts* (2010), the term paratext takes on a heightened relevance to transmedia franchises where numerous smaller texts (like the trailer analyzed earlier in this chapter) orbit the 'primary' text (the film or show) and inform audience expectations and experiences of it.

Though Gray's book slightly precedes the boom of streaming series, his distinction between two major types of paratexts is still relevant; he calls them 'entryway' and 'in medias res' paratexts. For Gray, entryway paratexts are those that are crafted to *precede* the primary text, or to prepare the viewer to open what he calls the text's 'airlocks' (a metaphor originally proposed by Genette) in order to 'control and determine our *entrance* into a text', while *in medias res* paratexts 'inflect or redirect the text following initial interaction' (Gray 2010: 35). Conventional examples of the former may be more intuitively familiar – movie reviews, media coverage, trailers, commercial tie-ins – whereas the latter often comes to fruition when secondary texts are created as *extensions* to the primary one. Gray uses the second category to broach similar philosophical topics that Jenkins confronts with his 'transmedia storytelling'– theorizing how consumers navigate the apparent 'overflow' of contemporary culture, where the onslaught of different possible connections between texts becomes hard to nail down with any sense of certainty (45). Even a basic chronology in the life of a franchise – how the 'primary' and 'secondary' texts are encountered – has become difficult to state. And as Gray admits, 'with texts alive interminably, forever open to toggling, paratexts may always exist *in medias res*' (ibid.), leading to a culture where we can speculate about reading practices where 'paratexts sometimes take over their text' (ibid.).

Gray's example is of a child who consumes a Happy Meal without ever seeing the movie that sponsored its tie-in toy (ibid.).

Whereas Gray's two categories of paratextuality are indeed helpful reminders of the knotty ways that a text can relate to its many subsidiaries, the eventual breakdown between them also demonstrates that the distinctions he proposes are fluid and depend on individual choice. Moreover, the indeterminate language Gray uses also anticipates a film like *The Spider-Verse*, which a decade later not only presupposes, but takes full advantage of this fluidity, using the various practices of interpretation and hierarchy as the starting point for its creative approach to identity politics in popular culture. Here then the term hypertext is helpful to delineate how an individual film like *The Spider-Verse* can itself represent and even theorize a relationship between imagined paratexts, making the hierarchy of different entries an analogue for its hero's journey into adulthood.

Though this book uses the term not in any new sense per se, it does so as a way to highlight both the theoretical features of the film's narrative, and to evoke the nervous, propulsive experience of watching *The Spider-Verse*, which thrives on a seemingly endless – call it hyperactive – capacity to build on its own auto-referential energy, as if to respond knowingly to the insights of recent academic studies of live-action *Spider-Man* paratexts (Gilmore 2017). Moreover, while the film's density of visual and sonic references may resemble other recent youth-oriented films and streaming series (especially those mentioned previously from Marvel Studios), its capacity for autoreferentiality also attempts something more ambitious, by entwining those same hypertextual features with a practical concern for representation – in this case, an attempt to capture the authentic experience of a multiracial teenager trying to access a character already ensconced in multiple generations of white hypotext.

Diversity in the Multiverse

One of the notable ways in which Spider-Man has endured for generations in popular culture is through his malleability. For decades, both licensed and unlicensed versions of the web slinging hero have populated different languages and cultures across the globe, animating the imaginations of youthful readers and viewers everywhere. It is rare, however, that mainstream evocations of Peter Parker acknowledge the essential porousness – and plurality – of his popularity, and how diverse youth audiences might also identify with a white teenager whose appeal derives from a mask that renders him fruitfully anonymous – allowing for the proliferation of what Stuart Hall would call 'negotiated' readings for people who can imagine themselves 'behind the mask' (Hall 1980).

Recently, Marvel and DC Comics both have adopted 'multiverse' storylines where multiplicity becomes a feature rather than a bug. The first successful use of the conceit in comics apparently dates to *Flash* issues of the 1970s, where the hero used his speed to access other dimensions – a narrative premise that animates the hero's return to screens in *The Flash* (Muschietti, 2023). As Jeffrey Brown suggests, the sheer pacing and market sensitivity of comic book publishing over the decades ensures that numerous different illustrators and writers become responsible for the same characters over time, which makes super-heroes and their stories by nature 'splintered, contradictory and mercurial' (2021: 18). In terms of Spider-Man, Brown notes, a specifically multi-dimensional 'Spider-Verse' was first marketed for comics in 2014–15 with a 'massive crossover event' spanning numerous series and storylines, valorizing dozens of new Spider-People as part of the Marvel family of possible Spider-People – 'from Cowboy Spider-Man, to Cyborg Spider-Man, to Cosmic Spider-Man, to even Spider-Monkey' (17). The goal of expanding the canon in this way was not simply to be humorous, but rather to create opportunities for 'multiple female variations […] as well as a range of ethnic and national variants such as Spider-Men who are African American, Indian, Latino, Japanese and Chinese' (18).

In a class handout that he posted on his blog shortly after the publication of *Convergence Culture*, Jenkins condenses his argument by pointing to ten key features of transmedia storytelling, while also specifying more about the uncertain ground between entries that are at once 'self-contained' and offering a 'point of entry 'for other texts. He writes:

> The encyclopaedic ambitions of transmedia texts often result in what might be seen as gaps or excesses in the unfolding of the story: that is, they introduce potential plots which cannot be fully told or extra details which hint at more than can be revealed. Readers, thus, have a strong incentive to continue to elaborate these story elements, working them over through their speculations, until they take on a life of their own. Fan fiction can be seen as the unauthorized expansion of these media franchises into new directions which reflect the reader's desire to 'fill in the gaps' they have discovered in the commercially produced material.
>
> (Jenkins 2007)

In citing 'gap filling' as a key exercise, Jenkins invokes an entire history of narrative theory and adaptation studies prior to the appearance of his work. He also points the way toward much of his later research, which focuses on the 'participatory cultures' and activism of fan communities, theorizing the different ways that audiences make collective meaning from the commercial products that surround them (Jenkins 2006; 2009). Moreover, his description alludes to the importance of 'speculations' and 'unauthorized expansion' – two different ways of referring to the remit of another field – fan studies – which over the past thirty years has become even more fascinated with the manifold 'decoding' processes provided by internet platforms (Hall 1980).[3]

As superhero franchise films have surged to a dominant form in the 2000s and 2010s, secondary texts have proliferated in their wake, many of them positioned to comment on the 'main' films from Disney and Warner Bros. Due to its animation, subject matter, and more modest distribution, *The Spider-Verse* could be seen as one of these secondary forms – a position that arguably allows the film more provocative critical latitude. James C. Taylor analyzes it from this perspective, placed alongside other recent animated films – *The LEGO Batman Movie* (Chris McKay, 2017) and *Teen Titans Go! To the Movies* (Aaron Horvath and Peter Rida Michail, 2018) – and argues that animated superhero films use their 'subordinate status' to 'critically reflect on their live-action counterparts and the broader network of parallel universes in which they are situated' (2021b: 87). For Taylor, the distinction between the animated films and the live action ones is primarily attributed to the use of parody. In the case of *The Spider-Verse*, the appearance of so many 'Spider-People' creates a spectrum of tonal representations that makes the prospect of a multiracial humanoid webslinger just one of many options. While some critics like Dru Jeffries point out that the film thereby contorts the true history of Spider-Man cartoons, which were much later to include equitable racial representations (a 2000s phenomenon) than they were others (some of which date to the 1960s) (Jeffries 2022: 195), Taylor argues that this risk of ahistoricism is at least balanced by the ways in which the film's collage of possibilities manages to affirm difference rather than simply represent it on the surface.

Yet with the popularity of *The Spider-Verse*, the film also managed to emerge out of its presumed secondary status to challenge the representational stakes of the more dominant 'mothership' franchise films. And as the film eventually garnered the Oscar for Best Animated Feature, the multiverse conceit became a hinge point for its reception in terms of racial representation. In his recent assessment of this terrain,

Brown argues that the placement of Miles at the center of a familiar white heroic story makes him a welcome alternative to other recent superhero films, where racial and ethnic identity are at the very core of the character's heroism and origin story. To the contrary, writes Brown, 'while Miles' ethnicity is significant, it does not mark him, or qualify him, as a lesser variation of a presumed "real" Spider-Man' (2021: 29). In other words, Miles will not just be yet another alternative who reaffirms the centrality of his 'real' white predecessor. Instead, his character will supersede Parker, not once but twice. The first Peter (the blonde one voiced by Chris Pine) dies in the opening act, killed by the Kingpin and delegating a callow Miles to replace him with his final gasp. The second Parker – this one identified as 'Peter B.' – arrives when the Super Collider breaks down. Peter B.'s paunch and brown hair mark him as different from the initial Peter, and he is also relegated to a secondary role, a wisecracking side kick and occasional mentor for our new hero rather than the customary protagonist.

In contrast with most other film versions thus far, *The Spider-Verse* is notable for how it embraces its central character in a way that evokes its own dynamics of what Mark J.P. Wolf would call the 'subcreation' of a character (2012). Miles Morales was first created by Marvel under the guidance of writer Brian Michael Bendis to explicitly cater to more racially diverse youth audiences. For Bendis, already a notable comic book writer at both DC and Marvel by that time in his career, these matters became notably more personal when he and his wife adopted two daughters in 2011 – one African American and the other Ethiopian. At that same moment, Marvel was engaged in a public relations effort to relate its products to Black and Latinx audiences. Kathryn Frank documents how that effort met with a series of social media conflagrations during the pre-production phase of several Marvel live action films in the early 2010s, as some fans questioned the casting of Black actors in roles that had been white in their comic originals (Idris Elba as Heimdall in *Thor* and Michael Clarke Duncan as the Kingpin in *Daredevil*) (Frank 2016: 246–7).

Later that same year, Miles Morales was introduced as part of the *Ultimate Spider-Man* comic book series, quickly becoming a key cog in the emergent Marvel 'multiverse' of the late aughts and early teens, which aimed to rewrite iconic superheroes that could empower a more diverse readership. As Frank points out, the initial version of Miles that appeared in *Ultimate Fallout* and the subsequent comics series, engineered by Bendis and artist Sara Pichelli in 2012, met with mixed reviews. Many readers appreciated the effort to include a Black Spider-Man in the canon, but some bristled at the way in which race became the central tenant of Miles' story arc – to the point that his place as an 'alternative' to Peter Parker became a defining negative character trait rather than any positive difference from the white norm (Frank 2016: 217).[4]

As *The Spider-Verse* attained greater visibility, winning the Oscar in 2019, critics immediately noted its novelty, pointing to its distinction from other high profile superhero films that dealt with the issue of race. Most proximate in memory at the time was *Black Panther*, which earlier in the previous year drew raves along similar lines. But that film was different, both because it was live action and because it treated race and ethnicity as integral to the hero's fictionalized African identity. *The Spider-Verse*, on the other hand, sought something more universal, centering Morales as more than a mere racialized alternative to Peter Parker. *New York Times* critic Peter Debruge put it succinctly: 'Miles' background is a nonissue [...] the takeaway here is anybody can be Spider-Man – and that's a revolutionary idea for a generation of kids eager to identify with Marvel's most popular superhero (quoted in Brown 2021: 29). The perceived universality of the cinematic Miles was also notably different than the initial reception of his appearance in the comics. As co-authors Trevor Boffone and Christine Herrera put it in a book tracking the trajectory of recent Latinx representation in popular culture, *The Spider-Verse* manages to 'normalize the Afro-Latino adolescent experience in a subtle way; that is, by not drawing excessive attention to things like Miles's code-switching or his last name, these aspects become refreshingly normal, simply a part of who he is' (Boffone and Herrera 2022: 63).

A significant part of the success of the film in this regard lies in the ways that its provocations in terms of race are wrapped in hypertextual packaging. In other words, the logic of the diversity presented in *The Spider-Verse* is first and foremost one of style, as the film uses the language of film adaptation and technological remediation to foster visual and sonic metaphors that offer multiple possible entry points, and therefore flexible reading positions to different audience members. More recent literature on transmedia tackles the relationship between formal features and representation. What if multimedia franchises, despite their plural entry points, still perpetuate systems of racial inequity? In response to these questions, Jenkins and other theorists have expanded on their ideas to consider how the changing formal relationships between media texts foster other power dynamics in their reception and modes of representation.

In some cases, multimedia artists have also provided a helpful example. In an analysis of transgender multimedia artist Janelle

Monáe, for instance, Dan Hassler-Forrest shows how Monáe's creative work resists the pull of centralized storytelling techniques on all fronts, instead distributing the elements of their story world (the eponymous 'WondaLand') across music and videos, but also in concept art for albums, concerts, and other public appearances (2017: 377). For Monáe, a resistance of a normative storytelling technique that is itself so multi-faceted involves the refusal to dictate a particular viewing order or hier-archy of meaning within their various modes of communication. Drawing on their example from concept albums like *The ArchAndroid* (2010) and *Dirty Computer* (2018), Hassler-Forrest argues that Monáe's practice constitutes a *heteroglossic* approach to storytelling across media – one that allows for viewers to encounter a polyphony of voices simultaneously and in no particular order (380). Rather than the cen-tripetal pull of a mothership, Monáe's is a 'centrifugal' use of transme-dia that resists the normative power of pulls toward any center, allowing for a multiplicity of reading strategies and for a more unfocused form of reception of different voices from within (382).

For *The Spider-Verse*, the tension between what Hassler-Forrest terms 'centripetal' and 'centrifugal' narration arguably becomes an organizing principle. The reasons for this are multiple, extending to nearly every stage of the film's conception and production. For one, the idea for *The Spider-Verse* was itself a combination of studios – Sony and Marvel – that had been engaged in a push-and-pull negotiation for years regard-ing rights to the character. These prolonged negotiations and eventual truce led to a unique set of circumstances allowing the directorial trio of Perischetti, Lord, and Miller remarkable latitude for an improvisational writing style and multi-stage animation process that took four years to complete. In terms of narrative, the explosion of the Kingpin's Super Collider causes secondary worlds to collapse and merge into one another, propelling new Spider-characters into Miles Morales' Brooklyn home world and setting up his quest for personal identity as measured against every order of possible aesthetic difference.

During the film, a lot of this journey occurs at the level of filmic expression itself. Sequences of the action are routinely interrupted by conventions of comic books – thought bubbles, gutters, and splash pages that evoke the film's plurality of generic origins. Above and beyond this level of cross-pollination, the film's animation is also ren-dered with a constant trembling, imperfect quality, suggesting a layer of uncertainty added to its generic origins. Finally, while the 'trans-media' effects felt here are not actually conceived across multiple plat-forms (as with Jenkins' *Matrix* example), this is a film that in many ways *internalizes* the stakes of media proliferation, rendering them visible and tactile for a presumed spectator who is already sensitive to these processes. By introducing the multiverse conceit in its storytelling and animation techniques, *The Spider-Verse* beckons the viewer 'into' a similar mode of questioning the stakes of representation.

Take, for instance, the continual 're-introduction' of characters discussed at the opening of this chapter. In the organization of the film, the previously described 'My name is ...' sequence becomes a recurrent signpost for the film, which leverages increasing audience familiarity with the same stylistic patterns to gradually invoke new artistic and conceptual dimensions of the film's multiverse. Notably, a very similar (though briefer) montage arrives with Peter B. (voiced by Jake Johnson), the erstwhile, now thirtysomething version of the web-slinger from Earth-616 (his most common home in the comics). When Peter B. arrives in *this* film's primary world (Earth-1610), it is due to the malfunctioning of the villainous Kingpin's Super Collider device, which motivates stylistic disruptions. This time though, details are signposted with differences for the viewer to recognize: a blue (rather than red) 'My name is' badge and, notably, a more faithful replica of the kissing scene from Raimi's *Spider-Man*, positioning Peter upside down. The internalized comparisons between the two Peter Parker sequences facilitate more of the same later, so that when Miles' school crush, Wanda (Hailee Stanfield), is revealed as Spider-Gwen, she gets her own abbreviated version of the same montage, as do the three lesser Spider-sidekicks – Spider-Man Noir (Nicolas Cage), Peni Parker (Kimiko Glenn), and Spider-Ham (John Mulaney). By this point, the grammar of the introductory montage is so familiar that the three origin stories are presented simultaneously on a subdivided, three-paneled screen evoking comic books (see Figure 1.2).

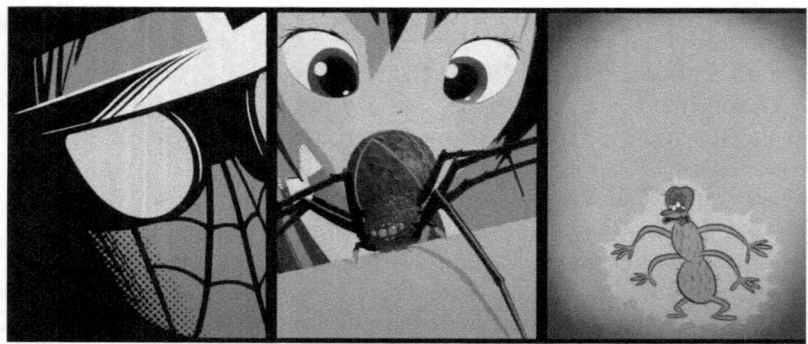

Figure 1.2 Three origin stories occur simultaneously in different panels

Arguably, the repetition of these elements, here in a parodic format, also encourages audience defamiliarization from them all. While those viewers already acquainted with the diversity of different possible Spider-People across the comics will have occupied this position, the film now assures that relative 'unknowing' audience members will also reach a similar place, able to distinguish the 'My name is …' montage as a mere, repeated formal exercise rather than a storytelling technique – one where a caricatured cartoon pig emerges, shoulder to shoulder with humanoid heroes.

Conclusion

In the context of a film that already encourages so much stylistic awareness and narrative flexibility, racial and ethnic diversity become just two of the many possible differentiating elements to track on screen. So when Miles finally has his own 'Let's do this one last time' montage near the end, his proclamation that he is the 'only' Spider-Man no longer bears the weight of upending an entire tradition of characters, nor the pressure of living up to a singular representation. In this way, the film allows Miles to retain markers of his ethnic identity without making them the hinge point of his character development. Despite their significant contributions, earlier landmark films like *Boyz n the Hood* (John Singleton, 1991), *Menace II Society* (Hughes brothers, 1993), or *Stand and Deliver* (Ramon Menéndez, 1988) often struggled to showcase underrepresented groups while also avoiding the insensitive shorthand of cultural cliché. Perhaps because he arrives several screen generations later than these important predecessors, Miles instead manages to be a character who simply *is* multiracial, and for whom cultural experiences seem more like factual reality than a leveraged marketing strategy. For it is Miles, the film's new protagonist, who is the reason for the multiverse conceit – a teen just unassuming and skittishly charismatic enough to offer a direct contradiction to Peter's winking proclamation that 'There can be *only one* Spider-Man'. And in the final sequence, nearly the same narration and montage will once again repeat, this time announced triumphantly by an Afro-Latino youth who asserts his place as the 'only' Spider-Man. Claiming a title that has eluded him for most of the film, Miles exclaims that if he can do it, 'anyone can wear the mask'.

As should be clear by now, Peter's opening catchphrase – 'let's do this one last time' – is purposefully ironic, but also invitingly pliable. Within seconds of that invitation, we know that the film we are watching proposes neither *one* authoritative version of events nor any *last* accounting of them, but rather an opening for an entirely new version of known events to unfold. In so doing, *The Spider-Verse* encourages an active thought process about not only Spider-Man, but also about the nature of the present transmedia environment and its ramifications for contemporary youth culture. The chapters ahead further work to describe how the remarkable surface energy of *The Spider-Verse* layers in other provocative forms of meaning. Indeed, picking apart how the features of the film work moment-by-moment shows not only a propulsive, hyperactive momentum – but a rhetorical structure that supports a fragile form of social commentary about the status of minority youth cultures in America.

Notes

1 Perhaps the most assiduous member of this group is Dan Gvozden, co-host of *The Amazing-Spider-Talk* podcast and frequent contributor of 'Easter Egg' lists to the *Hollywood Reporter*. His list for *Into the Spider-Verse* stands as the most detailed and complete of a genre, which has proliferated on blogs and YouTube, especially in the era of the MCU's popularity. See Gvozden (2018).
2 For a useful history of the term, see Scolari (2019).
3 Jenkins' *Textual Poachers: Television Fans and Participatory Culture* (1992) preceded *Convergence Culture* (2006) and laid groundwork for numerous later studies of fans, which have accelerated and diversified over the past two decades. For additional reading on the emergent field, see Hills (2002); Gray, Sandvoss, and Harrington (2007); Scott and Click (2017); Pande (2020); Booth and Williams (2021).
4 A more extended discussion of racial representation in the comics and the film is in Chapter 3 of this book.

2 Animating the Spider-Verse
'This could literally not get any weirder'

From the jump, *Spider-Man: Into the Spider-Verse* (Bob Perischetti, Peter Ramsey, and Rodney Rothman, 2018) offers a sort of thought experiment for the audience. In this collective, imaginative journey into various permutations of the Spider-Possible, stylistic multiplicity is so central to the film's premise, so overt in its trailers and ad campaigns, that even those viewers unacquainted with any other Marvel films (or their comic book source material) come to understand that going *into* the Spider-Verse, as proposed by the title, means accepting explicit violations of the spatiotemporal constraints found in most filmmaking. Tracking with this self-aware address, the characters are frequently and conspicuously aware of potential viewer disorientation, often acknowledging it with humorous side comments. As Peter B. Parker puts it in response to the arrival of three more Spider-People – Spider-Man Noir, Peni Parker, and Spider-Ham – 'This could literally not get any weirder'.

A substantial amount of the 'weirdness' that Peter observes about *The Spider-Verse* is experienced through visual style. Some of this is a product of the film's mode of production as a relatively out of the way title at Sony Pictures Animation that was not expected to attract audiences the way it eventually did. Though the film is officially credited with a trio of directors – Perischetti, Ramsey, and Rothman – all members of the team describe the workflow of the project as a collective endeavor, free of the hierarchies they have usually associated with Hollywood animation. The eventual three names emerged over time out of a lack of one named director, with each member contributing enough to one aspect of the film that he eventually ascended to share the top spot. This collaborative approach helped to foster the distinctive look of the film, which they repeatedly liken to making 'a living comic book'. Among the numerous interviews they conducted around the release of the film, the three directors and producers Phil Lord and Christopher Miller consistently cite two primary creative

DOI: 10.4324/9781003166962-3

aims. First, they wanted to use novel animation techniques to link their film to its comic book antecedents while standing apart from the mainstream CGI look of Pixar and its competitors. Second, they wanted to make sure that all their experimentation made sense within the emotional trajectory of their main character, giving visual expression to his arrival as a revisionist presence in American youth culture ('How "Spider-Man …' 2019).

What results is a movie that pushes the parameters of comic book-to-film adaptation on multiple stylistic levels. First, the animators purposefully rejiggered the conventional approach to computer graphic imagery (CGI) by using variable frame speeds and avoiding image-smoothing processes that had become an industry standard with the success of production studios like Pixar and DreamWorks in the 2000s. By doing so, *The Spider-Verse* creates a deliberately non-photo-realist approach that incorporates both 3D rendering and subtle components of comic book art. Here, instead of smooth surfaces evocative of phenomenal reality, we see the lightly ruddy texture of Ben-Day dots, hatch-marks, and apparent 'smudges' or misalignments, all used in various ways to grant dimension to the contours of objects on the screen. Second, after the 3D rendering process, each of the frames of the film was painstakingly animated over again, this time by superimposing hand-drawn, two-dimensional techniques on top of the images to give characters and surfaces a distinctive look and allow for the addition of other familiar comic art conventions. Third, and to a far more overt degree, the film's art design plays repeatedly with a two-dimensional, flat-looking graphic style that evokes comic book conventions in a more direct manner, using action lines, onomatopoeia, frames, gutters, thought balloons, and splash pages in more obvious ways to communicate different aspects of the story.

This chapter analyses these various layers of visual style in *The Spider-Verse* by showing how the film uses CGI to deploy a combination of the artistic conventions of both live-action filmmaking and comic books. To do so, the analysis uses the concept of 'remediation' – a term first proposed by media scholars John David Bolter and Richard Grusin (1999), and later repurposed by Drew Morton as a framework for discussing how comic book adaptations in contemporary Hollywood treat their origins in paneled narrative (2016). By moving swiftly back and forth between the recognizable conventions of comics, live-action film, and animated film, *The Spider-Verse* creates a viewing experience that makes a new Spider-Man's coming-of-age theme ('great responsibility') dovetail with a visual style that *itself* seems to be searching for new forms of artistic expression.[1] Analyzing how each of these levels works one by one helps to show how the film's formal features open space for more subtle provocations in its thematic content. Notably, an understanding of the hypertextual surface design of *The Spider-Verse* helps delineate how Miles' own artistic creations in the film – slap tagging and street art – come to signify his unique identity as a multiracial youth character.

Remediating the Spider-Verse

The Spider-Verse is obviously not alone in its endeavor to bring comic book art to Hollywood screens. As Alisa Perren and Gregory Steirer document, the 2000s brought about a new chapter in the relationship between the comic book industry and Hollywood cinema, one often characterized by a convergence of personnel and properties in ways that had previously eluded the industry (Perren and Steirer 2021: 1–8). That dynamic has now crested to the point that, in the mid-2020s, superhero films reign as the dominant form of American cinema, and especially so in the aftermath of pandemic lockdowns, with less-spectacular genres increasingly relegated to streaming menus. As the popularization of the films increases, so too does the academic literature on comic book adaptation, as scholars contemplate the many different ways that movies can approximate, extend, or expand upon the paneled forms of narration theorized by Scott McCloud in his classic trio of illustrated how-to books on comic book storytelling (1994; 2000; 2006). Most of the work, of course, gravitates toward the most visible movies, which tend to be live action and to depend on lavish costumes, green screens, and CGI post-production as their primary resources for bringing comics to the screen. In his recent book on comic book adaptation in American blockbuster filmmaking, Morton (2016) offers a sustained analysis of how blockbuster cinema of the 2000s and 2010s found an aesthetic language to deploy new technologies (computer graphic imagery) by repurposing and combining the effects of older ones (comic books and films). Borrowing a term from Bolter and Grusin, Morton argues that the way recent films use comic books should be understood as *remediation* (2016: 5–8). In the words of those earlier authors, this means that contemporary media '[present] themselves as refashioned and improved upon versions of old technology' (Bolter and Grusin 1999: 15). A return to the concept of remediation helps to clarify how *The Spider-Verse* might fit into a similar mold, albeit as an animated feature.

For Bolter and Grusin, remediation is always a dialectic between two apparent options – immediacy and hypermediacy. Immediacy, in this sense, refers to how new technology imitates a seemingly transparent experience of reality, while hypermediacy indicates how that same technology can instead amplify the distance between new and old forms (1999: 21–2). Most of Morton's examples in his argument derive from the way that computer graphics are used to remediate live action films like *The Matrix* and *Scott Pilgrim Vs. The World* (Wright, 2010), which repurpose comic book elements in different ways to appeal to audiences who are both familiar and unfamiliar with the tradition (2016: 21–40). One of the most frequent forms of immediacy has to do with a style that evokes a transparent – or apparently unmediated – relationship to reality. Bolter and Grusin make the argument that throughout the history of art, new technologies have taken over this mimicry of human perception (1999: 23). The irony, of course, is that no technology is free of limitations in this regard. So invariably, the aesthetic of transparency involves technologically bound thresholds. Morton discusses this less-explored aspect of remediation in an interview with Henry Jenkins, referring to Pixar's frequent imitation of camera techniques in CGI rendering (Jenkins 2017). His example there is *Wall-E* (Andrew Stanton, 2008), which despite access to graphics software that could more fully replicate the visual dimensions of phenomenal reality, instead imitates the visual limits of hand-filmed technique, carefully recreating the camera movements (tracks, pans, dollies) and cinematographic 'accidents' (variable focus, handheld movements, lens flares) that result from a human-created, camera-bound style (ibid.).

The multiverse conceit of *The Spider-Verse* was made visible in nearly all the promotional trailers for the film and was reflected in the chaotic first months of the project's development. Each of the cast of characters was carefully planned by the animators, and the look of the film's worlds reportedly preceded even the crafting of the screenplay – including the iconic 'leap of faith' scene where Miles jumps from a skyscraper, finally convinced of his new talents (Renfro 2020). The producers were exacting about what they wanted the film to look like even before they knew what it would be about. In the development stages, one animator – Alberto Mielgo – designed initial concepts for the cast of characters only to be let go in favor of the team that produced the first teaser trailer of the film ("'Spider-Man: Into ...' no date). That trailer was eventually tested with audiences at Comic Con and later attached to feature films, depicting the iconic 'leap of faith' scene without including any dialogue and before the script had even been written (Renfro 2020).

Eventually, the duo of Perischetti and Rothman emerged as the heads of development, with Rothman writing the first version of the screenplay. Soon they also realized that an additional voice would be needed to make the depiction of Miles ring truer to the African-American and Latinx experiences they were hoping to capture. That is when they found Ramsey, whose diverse portfolio of work as a storyboard artist ranged from a first break working with Francis Ford Coppola, to a key role on *Boyz in the Hood* (John Singleton, 1991), and later to numerous other high profile live action films of the 1990s and 2000s, before a move to animation in the late 2000s led to his directorial debut on DreamWorks' ambitious and visually striking *Rise of the Guardians* (2012). An African American native of South Central Los Angeles who worked his way from a childhood in the projects to success in the industry, Ramsey's combination of animation expertise and life experiences provided the production team incalculable wisdom in its efforts to portray the film's cultural texture (Breznican 2021).

Later, each of the film's six main characters were featured separately on promotional posters for the film's advertising campaign, which also sometimes featured a larger version of all six. Juxtaposed together, the different characters pay tribute to the texture of a film that proposes a new freedom from visual verisimilitude for the viewer. Josh Beveridge of ImageWorks headed up the film's animation department and describes how each of the minor Spider-People in the film was a result of months of playing with the simulation of different animation techniques. They included Spider-Man Noir – voiced by Nicolas Cage and very much a 'gritty dude from 1930s comics' whose black-and-white tones also include larger Ben-Day dots and starker shadows; Peni Parker, whose 'anime influenced world' Beveridge admits was a look he had to research before settling on minimal dialogue and a large robot sidekick; and Spider-Ham/Peter Porker, who 'is a cartoon', fights with oversized hammers and anvils (redolent of Warner Bros.), and who the team rendered to look as much like a two-dimensional character as possible ('How Animators Created ...' 2019). Working with production designer Justin K. Thompson, Beveridge and his crew took months to make sure that each of these three characters could cohabitate the scenic spaces of the screen.

Yet these overtly variable character styles also only make sense with respect to the baseline expectation laid down by the film's primary world, defined by its humanoid leads – Miles Morales, Gwen Stacy, and Peter B. Parker. Stacy and Parker, the directors point out, were not created with the same nostalgia as the three other characters since they were more important to the emotional trajectory of Miles, who was always meant to be the center of the story ('How "Spider-Man ..." 2019). In this sense, the Brooklyn that Miles Morales lives in prior to the spider bite could be said to offer – at least in the context of the film's other more ornate animated sequences – a level of 'normative' transparent immediacy. Yet, even in the more-or-less 'realistic' sequences of the film's opening passages, the animators sought to make a visual style that stood as a stark contrast to the Pixar method of immediacy as an analogue for filmed 'realistic' surfaces. The image track evokes this dynamic with its subtle references to the visual style of its source material. Beveridge describes Miles as their barometer here, and how the team used his world 'to establish the look of the film' as 'a hybrid between the look of 80s and 90s comics' which was 'not quite the printing techniques that they have today, because we wanted to take advantage of screen tones' ('How Animators Created ...' 2019). Notably, the film incorporates comic book aesthetics by using three identifiable techniques of computer imagery that draw inspiration from comic books.

The first of these techniques, half-toning, is a result of printing technology, which in comic books uses small, patterned circles – also called 'Ben-Day' dots – in different density patterns to create lighter shades that contrast with darker ones. In some cases, the printing process also smudges these distinctions a bit, falling just outside the lines of the figures drawn on the page, and signalling a second characteristic element – misprints common to a print-based medium. In *The Spider-Verse*, the visual effect of these apparent printing mistakes or 'chromatic aberrations' becomes a handy way for the filmmakers to acknowledge their debts to comic art while also adapting to filmic language. Using the smudged blur of color outside lines in gradated ways on a moving image, they give certain parts of the frame an out-of-focus look that also resembles the variable focus of a camera lens and the image's depth-of-field. The third technique, cross-hatching, derives from a more deliberate use of small lines that gives dimension to drawn figures by indicating shadows and contours.

As is evident in Figure 2.1, all three of these elements can be seen in turn – perhaps most clearly in the dimensions of ordinary mise-en-scène like the objects in Miles' bedroom ('How Animators ...' 2019). Notice, for instance, the box on his desk to the left, which acquires three-dimensional presence through the hatching on the right-hand side, and stands apart texturally from the desk below, itself graced with half-toning on different surfaces to create dimensionality. Likewise, the shelf, the poster on the wall, and Miles' drafting table all acquire further dimensionality through the slight smudging effects on their edges, which evokes the inexact misprints characteristic of comic book art (see Figure 2.1).

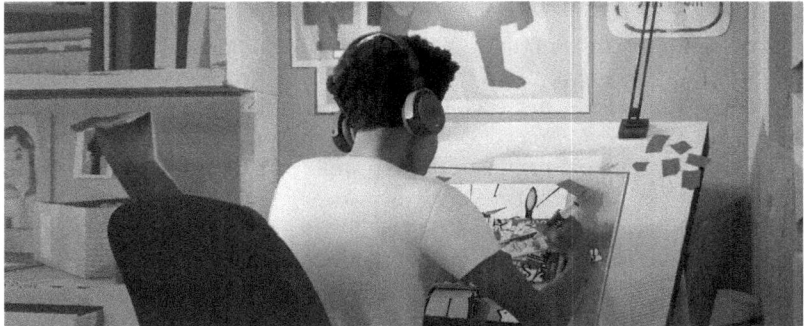

Figure 2.1 Miles is introduced working at his drafting table

In numerous places, these elements help define the edges of Miles and other characters. For instance, in Figure 2.2, half-toning is visible on Miles' forehead, alternating sizes of the circles in places to show shadows and variable light sources created by the morning and his father's flashing siren, which embarrasses him on the first day at Brooklyn Academy. Meanwhile, the background of the image achieves the look of being bathed in morning light through slight misalignments – the previously described 'misprints' – in the boxes that define the striations and shadowed ledges of the storefront located behind Miles. In this way, a comic book signifier is also used in *The Spider-Verse* to visually create an analogy with what in live action cinema would be termed depth-of-field. The adaptation game here thus moves in multiple directions in a single technique – from comic to animation to live action and back again.

Figure 2.2 Half-toning is visible on Miles' forehead

In addition to formal elements like colors and shapes, the film-makers sought to distinguish the quality of their moving images from other animated cinema they saw in the late 2010s. One of the primary ways they achieved this was to slow down the rate of images per second in the film. For decades, conventional animation has imitated the industry standard of live action filmmaking, which since the 1910s has adopted a standard rate of twenty-four frames of film per second of screen time – a practice colloquially referred to by animators as animating the film 'on ones'. Historically, reducing that number has been a way for animators around the world to distinguish their visual styles from others. Perhaps the most well-known example has been from Japanese artists like those of Studio Ghibli, which customarily has slower speeds, often twelve frames but sometimes as low as six frames per second ('on fours').

Throughout its runtime, *The Spider-Verse* varies these visual rhythms to its image track, using them thematically in places to distinguish between characters. The height of this creative aspect in terms of expressing the film's coming-of-age drama arguably occurs during a sequence later on, when Peter B. and Miles swing from tree to tree during their hasty retreat from the Alchemex lab, where they have just retrieved the technology necessary to fix the busted Super Collider. As they are pursued by Liv Octavius, the duo banter jovially about Miles' relative inexperience with his web shooters, and Peter B. teaches him how to use them. Meanwhile, as Peter B. instructs his protégé on technique ('whip and release!'), the animation combines movement speeds, putting the elder Spider-Man in a more traditional one ('on ones') while Miles is syncopated more slowly but in the same frame ('on fours'). Here then the learning process is expressed visually, as during the sequence Miles 'learns' his powers, and the animation technique redoubles his discovery, gradually bringing his character movements 'up to speed' to match his mastery of new skills.

In addition to these variable frame rates, Lord and Miller's team dispensed with some of the *de facto* realism of rendering technology that had become the norm in the 2010s.[2] One of these was the process of motion smoothing, which has become a built-in part of most computer graphic software. In this process, more frames of animation are artificially added to the image to make the movements of objects and characters on-screen look as close to three-dimensional, filmed reality as possible. Visually, the smoothing process makes movement look like a blur on the screen. However, the *Spider-Verse* team actively worked against these predilections of their own software, returning during the editing process to extract the automatic blurring effect out of sequences to replace it with their preferred smearing aesthetic – more associated with frame animation in the pre-CGI era. So the screen movement of Miles, his friends, and other objects in this film, while still animated in 3D, is engineered to leave more visible traces on the image track. This connection, evidenced by the apparent smearing of colors and lines, links their look not just to still comic book art, but also to the heritage of drawn animated frames more broadly.

On top of these important tweaks to 3D computer imagery, the animators wanted their film to retain visible connection to the hand-drawn legacies of comic books. That is why they added yet another layer of the process, which was to have hand-drawn elements of the image added on top of the generated sequences. This meant the painstaking process of creating a print of the 3D images and then re-animating every single frame by adding lines to emphasize and contour the features of characters and their surroundings. The result, however, is the dazzling 'shimmer' that the sequences get, many times imbuing them with a slightly mobile look. This effect is challenging to capture on the printed page, though close-up shots of characters provide more obvious places for the drawn lines as they appear, imposed on top of the blocks of color provided by CGI. Take for example the still below (see Figure 2.3), where Jefferson regards Miles in the rear-view mirror of his police cruiser. The concern lines on his forehead are here magnified in a way that helps distinguish more subtle features on his son's face behind. Notice also the distinction between the foreground (the reflection in the mirror) and the background, accomplished with half-toning and misprinting as discussed earlier. In motion, the cars meant to be out of focus acquire a smeared quality due to the slower frame speed.

Though these animation characteristics are subtle to the naked eye, they contribute collectively to the alternative look and feel of *The Spider-Verse*. Miller opines that the entire process of achieving this first layer of stylistic difference meant that in the initial stages, the team could only perfect one

Figure 2.3 Jefferson looks at Miles in his rear-view mirror

second of screen time per week of production – a significant reason for why the film took over four years to produce ('The Secrets Behind ...' 2019). Some of the other ways that *The Spider-Verse* leverages its comic book roots are far more overt in the film's visual design. That secondary level of the film's hypertextual visual style is the subject of the next section.

Hypermediacy

In many cases, the direct references to comic book art appear in a rhythm that is different from the immediacy effect of Miles' Brooklyn established earlier. They are common, for instance, in action scenes and montages. Sometimes, the result is not unlike a familiar effect in comic books, when splash pages are used to take over temporarily from the customary run of the narrative to dramatize the action of a character or, in many cases, a scene full of many characters at once. Scenes with clear split-screens are usually depicted with gutters – white borders of various sizes around the images. In some cases, these conventions take over the image field, functioning as a shorthand that summarizes previous events that the narrator is 'pretty sure you know'. Peter B. Parker, for instance, expresses a disdain for the familiarity of his heroics by glossing over them. To express this, the screen offers a series of different exploits in multiple subdivided panels, delineated with gutters. To add to the humor, the words 'Blah... blah... blah' appear mid-way through Peter's dialogue, superimposed over the different actions. The difference with comic books, of course, is that each of the eight panels here actually moves individually, and the three words (each separate 'Blah') arrives precisely when the sound of the word comes with the dialogue (see Figure 2.4).

Figure 2.4 Subdivided panels illustrate film dialogue by evoking comics

Action lines and onomatopoeia are also used as intermittent reminders of the comic book debts of *The Spider-Verse*. These are usually introduced in a staccato fashion, occupying the screen for less than a second in most cases. This occurs, for instance, during the sequence where Miles first begins to master his powers, swinging from building to building and leaping from car roof to car roof with exhilarating abandon. As he lands on one of the roofs, each time he deploys his next web from his hand, we get the word 'Thwip' written in stark white on the screen, along with diagonal lines that seem to issue from his hand along with the sound (see Figure 2.5).

Another one of these elements serves an important structural function in the narrative. When the Kingpin deploys his Super Collider, we see a sort of oozing mass of colored bubbles emanating from it, a strangely formless depiction of dimensional power that recurs any time the characters traipse into the spatiotemporally 'in-between' areas of the multiverse architecture mapped by the film's intrigue.

While uninitiated viewers could simply regard these shapes as part of the lexicon of this film, those familiar with comics will immediately recognize them as an homage to legendary illustrator Jack Kirby, who invented the style of 'Krackle' in his first comics work of the 1930s, developing it further over a six-decade career that spanned DC, Marvel, and most of their competitors.[3] Once revisualized as an element of actual moving pictures, this style becomes a multipurpose tool for the storytellers of *The Spider-Verse*. In some places, it enacts literal interruptions to the image track which, especially when accompanied by static sounds or other jumps on the soundtrack, may be experienced like actual projection glitches – as if the technology behind the film is itself experiencing instability. In the opening credits described above,

Figure 2.5 Text during an action scene evokes onomatopoeia

this creates a sort of lo-fi or unfinished feel in the imagery. Later, these interruptions become more integrated narratively, associated with the explosion of the Super Collider, which generates visible Krackle effects as part of the dimensional disruptions of its technology. The effect it has on the film is somewhat harder to capture in still images here, but eventually, in the logic of the story, references to Kirby become a visual rhetoric of sorts, cuing the viewer to recognize the pluralistic, indeterminate areas that lie between the more discrete dimensions of the multiverse from whence come Miles, Gwen, Peter B. and the other Spider-Folk.

Deriving from the apparent opposite side of the animation spectrum is the 'glitch' effect from the film. In the logic of the narrative, each of the Spider-People have moments when they seem to lose their foothold in Earth-1610. The film denotes these by superimposing a rapid series of angular shapes on top of the characters, combined with fluctuating shades of color. All of these effects are possible to create rather easily in the tools of basic editing software, as numerous YouTube content creators demonstrated when the 'Spider-Verse look' of animation began to have cultural currency after the release of the film.[4] As opposed to the smooth edges and clear comic book derivation of the Kirby Krackle, however, the hard edges and flickering visual quality of these triangle and quadrilateral shapes tend to create the feeling of a mistake or an error on the visual track, as if the movie itself is experiencing an instability of visual dimensions to go along with the narrative flux between primary and secondary fictional worlds. Like the opening 'My name is …' scene, these moments seem to suggest a basic instability of meaning – here linking the uncertainty of visual perception to the cascading referentiality of the events and images presented.

The Super Collider, of course, also provides the film with its primary narrative and thematic conceit, as its explosion is also what transports the five alternative Spider-People to the film's primary world. As Mark Minett and Bradley Schauer have argued, the idea of diverse heroes 'teaming up' has a long legacy in Marvel comics, dating back to the 'All-Star Team Books' that periodically brought different characters together for adventures alongside the mainline run of *Avengers* comics in the 1970s and 1980s (Minett and Schauer 2017). Building on this tradition, *The Spider-Verse* ups the ante by transporting different versions of the same character together in a narrative that involves battling against the very mechanics responsible for their unlikely collision in one world. They include Peter B., we learn, but also Gwen Stacy (also known as Spider-Gwen), Peter Porker (Spider-Ham), Spider-Man Noir (à la 1940s Hollywood) and Peni Parker (an anime-style girl who appears alongside her robot, SP//dr). Moments later, we learn, each of these Spider-People is also depicted as formally distinct from the others, drawn in art styles that seem mis-attuned with the verisimilitude as established by the 'immediacy' of Brooklyn on Earth-1610. So while the three primary humanoid personae (Peter B., Miles, Gwen) differ primarily in terms of age, gender, and race, the other three stretch generic credibility via aesthetics: Noir swoops down in stark black-and-white with a vocal track from Nic Cage doing his best Humphrey Bogart; Peni (Kimiko Glen) pops onto the screen, bathed in hearts and stars with pencil lines and halting movements reminiscent of anime; and Porker (John Mulaney) speaks with a vibrant lilt and sound effects that befit the more 'cartoonish' flatness of his appearance on-screen.

Finally, after each character is introduced, they interact in the primary world of the film, their respective animated styles often free to overlap and interact. At one point the image comes to rest on a memorable frame featuring all six characters side-by-side, forced into a collective Spidey-huddle on the ceiling of the dorm room Miles shares with his unsuspecting roommate (see Figure 2.6). The scene is reportedly the one that took the longest to animate in the entire film, perhaps because it brings together the diverse techniques that had to this point been used separately or in less complex combinations ('The Secrets Behind …' 2019).

By establishing a primary world where Ben-Day and smudges become familiar as this film's version of verisimilitude, the animators create a visual baseline – and a set of cues by which the viewer can make their own comparisons. Note that the primary humanoid characters – Miles, Peter B., and Gwen, roughly share the same aesthetic features, rendered three dimensional through the combination of

Figure 2.6 The main characters huddle together on the ceiling of Miles' dorm room

graphically-generated Ben-Day dots and hatch marks to provide shadow and proportion, along with hand-drawn lines to indicate detail work like their facial contours. The other three characters stand out here, largely because of their different aesthetics. Peni, with her anime-inspired *tareme* eyes and blushing cheeks, has more muted cell shading technique common to shadows in Japanese style. Noir, with his black-and-white palette and fedora, looks ripped directly from a world of low-key chiaroscuro, and Spider-Ham's thinly back-lit contours make his flatter, cartoony red-and-blue suit stand out even more starkly than they otherwise would. The backdrop of the room, meanwhile, appears bathed in night-time shadows thanks to the same misprint 'smudge' technique used to make previous passages look variable in their focus.

By adopting this novel 2D/3D approach to computer graphics, as well as inserting frames and sequences that imitate the narrative quirks and two-dimensional panel layout of comics, *The Spider-Verse* remediates the conventions of multiple art forms through the processes of CGI anima-tion. All these layers are, of course, difficult to grasp in real time – parti-cularly on a first viewing. Yet the film's most remarkable accomplishment may also lie in the way these complexities are integrated into the dynam-ics of narration, often used as a tool to comment on the larger thematic of Miles Morales' journey as a hero, his place as an alternative Spider-Man, and the representational dynamics that are the very basis of expanding the Spider-Man story to include an Afro-Latino protagonist.

Miles of Hypertext

The first chapter of this book made the case for how the 'My name is …' montage, first narrated by Peter Parker (Earth-616 version), provides a touchstone for how *The Spider-Verse* references other media objects. Likewise, early sequences of the film delineate the other visual layers, allowing later scenes to develop greater thematic connections between the primary world of Brooklyn (Earth-1610) and the secondary worlds of Gwen Stacy, Peter B. Parker, Spider-Man Noir, Peter Porker and Peni Parker. While the half-toning, Ben-Day dots, hatch marks, and smudged coloring techniques discussed earlier do contribute a subtle comic book veneer to Miles, his friends, and his animated home, the fateful spider bite triggers another level of complexity – a cascade of visual changes that are linked more obviously to the conventions of panel illustration. As the look, feel, and rhythm of the images change, moving from a cultivated sense of transparent immediacy to a more obviously hypermediated style, they also multiply possible meanings, both in complementary and con-tradictory ways. The contrast between these two approaches is used early to depict Miles' own creative appropriation of his environment and draw visual distinctions between the types of cultural production that will later come to signify his internal search for meaning.

Miles is first introduced to the audience at the end of (the blonde) Peter Parker's 'My name is …' montage. 'There's only one Spider-Man', Peter quips, winking confidently at the audience while he flips in the air, 'and you're looking at him'. Cut to an extreme closeup of two brown-hued hands completing work on what appears to be a pile of different colored corporate name tags resembling the one featured earlier in Peter's narration. This time, though, the name tags are repurposed as slap tags with the name 'Miles' on them, stacked on top of one another on his drafting board in a way that obscures their specific features. Closer scrutiny reveals a red 'Hello' tag with the letters '-les' (apparently the final three letters in 'Miles') and several others buried lower in the pile – including one that appears to be in Spanish rather than English (the word 'Hola' is clearly visible near the bottom). At the center, though, is a darker blue tag that the hands appear to be actively working to shade in with a yellow highlighter (see Figure 2.7).

The animators are on record about their intentions with this scene, which was meant to make Miles relatable and 'lovable' by showing that he is 'capable of creating without feeling self-conscious or encumbered'. They also point out that 'everything is a microcosm for something larger' (Rothman and Lord, quoted in Harris 2019). While Lord and Rothman are mostly referring to the details that were already in the screenplay about how Miles would be presented, the sequence as it appears in its final version also functions as a sort of introduction to how they will use the split between layers of possible meaning as depicted in the animation. Miles experiments with different ways to

Figure 2.7 Miles' tag design connotes multiple origins

introduce himself, but while the layered name tags in his notebook offer a clue about his own search for identity, they also associate that identity with the act of image-making itself. Notably, the frame here also provides the film's first clear distinction between those features that are immediate and hypermediate. The hands here are given dimension with the shadows and smudging provided from the varied rendered textures of Ben-Day dots, whereas the lines and nails of the skin are brought out via the use of second-layer, hand-drawn lines. That distinction is then redoubled by the tag design that Miles seems to be working on here, itself the product of shading (the yellow highlighter) and drawn lines (apparently in black pen). Already then, we see the split between visual features of animation that are transparent and immediate. Miles' hands, his markers, and the name tags are presented as diegetic facts – products of the transparency of the animation, but not questioned as such. Meanwhile, in the same frame, the act of creation that Miles does here draws attention to the process of shading and hand-drawn lines *that he is creating himself* – the same two layers that the viewer has likely overlooked for the sake of that same immediacy in the scene's verisimilitude.

The single image in Figure 2.7 thus activates both the immediacy of the visual style of Miles' 'reality' and demonstrates its main visual components in how he crafts his slap tags. There are other elements, however, that are less readily readable. Most notable in this sequence is the word that Miles is configuring on the dark blue tag – his artistic signature, with the name 'Miles' subtly contained in the loops inside the round 'O' shapes. Though it is prominently displayed in the center of the frame, the bubbly form of the letters and their variable sizes make the word difficult to process on one pass. Two halves of the quotation marks on the word appear to be disguised versions of the numbers '20' and '18', hence a reference to the year of Miles' story (and the film's release). The word between those marks is less readable, with a second 'o' on the end possibly suggesting an extended form of the word – 'oiloo!' Inscrutable at first glance, this apparent neologism in bubble letters also arguably bares traces of Miles' multilingual heritage. The word itself, though hardly obvious, could constitute an alternative or slang spelling of the common Spanish exclamation 'oye!' – roughly translated as 'hey' and often used to mean 'look at that' or 'listen to this'. In the context of everyday usage, 'oye' should also be understood as an expression of surprise, incredulity, or eyerolling disbelief. Moreover, the fact that it is not entirely legible or translated bespeaks not only the dynamics of most street art and slap tagging, but also to another layer of linguistic complexity having to do with the multilingual reality that Miles lives in – where the double o's at the end of his invented word, hiding his name, also suggest the beginning of the English language 'look'. The tagging signature here is thus linguistically and visually ambivalent – with a potential English meaning obscured by an apparent layer of Spanish expression, and vice versa.

The seconds that follow perform a similar demonstration of immediacy and hypermediacy, this time with regard to movement in the frame. At the beckoning of his parents, Miles hurriedly prepares for his first day at Brooklyn Visions Academy, the fancy new high school he will be attending across town. While the narrative content of these opening moments may seem straightforward, the amount of information communicated here is also remarkably condensed. He closes his notebook, revealing briefly what appears to be another sketch of a robot on his drafting table. As he bursts into the living space of the Morales apartment, a flurry of activity ensues, mimicking various forms of verisimilitude common to live action filmmaking. The frame 'dollies' back through a doorway, revealing off-screen space in an animated rendition of deep focus cinematography, while depicting a shift in family dynamics in bustling, spatial terms. *Citizen Kane's* (Welles, 1941) iconic boyhood scene seems distantly relevant here, among so many others, but audiences are never given pause to make many such analogies due to other perceptible features of the animation. As Miles darts screen left, then back to center frame, gathering his school supplies and avoiding his parents, the forms that crisscross the space move differently than most films, animated with fewer 'frames' (drawings) per second than the customary speed 'on ones'.

While most viewers may perceive but cannot specify the reasons for this variable speed, the animation interjects other minute visual cues to mark its aesthetic distance from the depth cues of filmed live action provided by the techniques discussed earlier. Perhaps most obviously, Miles nearly collides with his mother in the kitchen doorway, causing her to spill her tea, and the collision and its aftermath are dramatized through jagged, hand-drawn action lines on the top left-hand side of the image (see Figure 2.8).

Figure 2.8 The Morales family prepares for their day

This sequence thus offers the audience a remediation of elements through a combination of comic book and live action conventions. While the collision results in the conventional marks of an explosion recognizable in comic book terms, the sequence also carefully displays a diversity of options, setting them off against the conventions of a second technological resource. The background attains both depth and a feeling of variable focus through the misprint aesthetic and smudging of edges. Moments later, as Miles shovels down breakfast cereal, he also seems to smell scents wafting from cooking on the stove. As he lifts a pot lid from slightly off-screen, curvy lines emanate upwards, graphically indicating a pleasurable smell as he slightly burns his mouth on hot soup. The connotation of fragrant home-cooked food is one of a jumble of signifiers that help the film to capture the quotidian, multi-ethnic Morales household, which also functions as a combination of cultural elements. Jefferson speaks English while Rio speaks Spanish. Miles, their multiracial son, code switches between the two languages as the three animated bodies move frantically on the screen around one another, preparing for the workday.

While the directors wanted to ensure these various cultural details were received by the audience, they also wanted them to appear without feeling forced (DuVernay 2019). This is also true of the sequence that follows. Miles hugs his mother on the front stoop of their building, navigates the sidewalks and streets of his neighborhood while greeting other teenagers. Evoking the glide and slight bounce of handheld technique, the frame follows Miles on his way, stopping and turning at variable distances. A flurry of conversations ensues from passers-by ('We miss you, Miles!'; 'How is that new school?') as the camera again mimics live-action filming techniques. Other greetings are via slapped hands and nods, which generate their own hand-drawn action lines, each appearing for a split second. Meanwhile, the smudges of the misprint aesthetic designate the visual depths of a vibrant neighborhood, presented as naturalistic, much like the multilingual banter, which flows from English to Spanish and back again. Miles skips joyously down the block, slapping the tags we saw him create in the previous scene onto various available surfaces – a swinging ATM sign, a newspaper box. He then leaps and a close-up shot shows his hand affixing the aforementioned 'Oijoo!' tag on a distinctively Brooklyn street sign – Wythe Avenue (see Figure 2.9).

Again, imitating the variable depth-of-field of live-action filming technique, the background row houses are rendered here with a smudge/misprint style while the road sign stays in sharp foreground

Figure 2.9 Small details count on this street sign

focus. Meanwhile, the sign is also endowed with another notable detail, as a second viewing reveals another sticker on the sign that looks to offer an English translation of the Spanish tag Miles has placed there – 'Loook'. Miles subsequently trips over his shoelace on the curb, falling in front of his father's police cruiser. Jefferson picks him up, takes him to school, and embarrasses him by loudly demanding he tell him that he loves him in front of numerous new classmates on the front steps of Visions Academy. In addition to offering a well-nigh universal trope of the teen experience – public embarrassment at the behavior of parental figures – these first few sequences all share, the same visual approach, using comic book visual style in a manner that replicates the immediacy of filmed camera technique, perceptibly different than Pixar, but not radically so. Meanwhile, on another level, all of these disparate elements combine to offer a universal of youth experience and the teen film: eye-rolling embarrassment around parents.

The relative transparency of these sequences is starkly contrasted just a few minutes later. Miles goes to visit his Uncle Aaron that evening. The sequence begins with a close-up of Aaron dropping the needle on his turntable, which cues the opening beats of 'Hypnotize' by The Notorious B.I.G. These passages of the image track are filled with signifiers of a different Brooklyn, which appears here in low-lit visuals, dusk providing the motivation for a murkier color palette punctuated by new stimuli like the brightness of car headlights and Biggie's famous lyrics ('… timbs for my hooligans in Brooklyn …'). Aaron and Miles, we learn, are complicit in their love of the urban environs, and Aaron leads his nephew on a night-time adventure, down alley ways and over chain-link fences to a vaulted, underground sanctuary in the subway. The depths of the underground are ideal for unsanctioned spray painting. Yet as these sequences unfurl, the visual style also gradually begins to change, eschewing the active frame mobility of previous scenes for a more static, geometric approach. Not only that, but as Aaron watches Miles paint his graffiti response to the school's assigned reading – *Great Expectations* – a furtive spider arrives, strangely also pulsing with light, making its way under Miles' jacket.

No accident that in this film's iteration of the famous spider-bite episode, layers of media consumption are again evoked visually. This time, the film frames them as a literal act of remediation. As Miles pauses to photograph his handiwork with his cell phone, the screen's vivid version of the artwork gets a frame-within-a frame treatment. Screen-left, the image on his phone offers an embedded layer of meaning (diegetic digital reproduction) that overlays the transparent immediacy of the one viewers have already been tracking (the flat wall of graffiti art and simulated 'rack focus' effect of Miles' foregrounded profile). Dickens' classic is rendered visible here in multiple layers, as Miles (this world's Pip) records evidence of his own creation via the 'clarifying' digital reproduction of an image that is already a self-aware comic book homage (see Figure 2.10).

Here, not only does the frame of the cell phone's viewfinder provide a condensation of the larger painting on the wall, but it also redoubles, albeit in slight altered form, the layered look of the previous frame on Miles' drafting table. Moreover, the frame of the cell phone screen also momentarily gives us a frame-within-a-frame, marking off the smaller version of the painting against the softer rendition of the same artwork on the subway wall. One frame encapsulates both the narrative and thematic layers involved in remediating an icon of youth culture.

Figure 2.10 Miles captures his creation

Soon after the spider bite, these elements bleed into the continuity of the images without plausible, realistic explanation, while also adding a more explicit connection to comic book conventions. The motivations for their inclusion are simultaneously subjective and supernatural, as Miles' transformative powers turn his internal thoughts into what narrative theorists of film adaptation might call a 'mindscreen' wherein comic book thought bubbles graft themselves on top of a moving image rather than a still one. In the context of a moving film image, these balloons become both a visual interruption and a sonic continuity with the voiceover, as the insecurities of the character are brought graphically to the fore (see Figure 2.11).[5]

When Miles enters Visions Academy, he becomes aware of his new powers, but also (apparently?) of the 'loud' visual interruptions created by the onslaught of yellow boxes that appear on-screen next to him. The ambiguity of possible interpretations, of course, is never resolved one way or another. Rather, the cause of Miles' reaction dwells somewhere in the uncertain space of the remediation process itself. Thought boxes – staples of comic art – arrive on top of the more 'immediate' filmic conventions, and could plausibly be sourced to Miles' gradually encroaching superpowers (his Spidey sense increases the volume of nearby conversations), to the sudden accommodation of comic book logics in his reality (bold yellow thought balloons invade the visual field), or to some uncertain combination of the two and how they combine in the visual fold. It is here, then, that we get an example of how the film constitutes a dialogic between different forms of what Morton would call 'stylistic remediation', smartly embedded within the mechanics of possible interpretation. Put differently, *The Spider-Verse* does not ever work to resolve the mixture of plausible graphic

Figure 2.11 Loud voices erupt in Miles' head

meanings offered. Instead, it wraps several possibilities into the image itself, packaging their resolution into the hero's journey. Miles' quest to reconcile his place in the world – or to balance his Spidey senses with the other dimensions of his life – becomes inseparable from the graphic confrontations between the diverse conventions and art styles of different media. These tensions reach a fever pitch moments later, as Miles' paranoid misgivings about the 'loud' conversations (in his head or on the screen?) will splash into a full-fledged 'page' on the movie screen, no longer contained by scripted thought bubbles as before (see Figure 2.12).

It is important that the splash page here superimposes Miles on top of it, but in a way that retains his 3D shading and styling, separating his body from the images and gutters that are behind him, and granting them a further 2D look by visual comparison. Moreover, while they are more mimetic than the impressionistic contours of the street art seen prior, the frames here are impossible to read independently, especially since they are only isolated body parts, couched in a pastel color scheme that further separates from the objective world of Visions Academy. Rather, they register as a compilation of different partial view – furtive eyes, a mocking smile, a laughing mouth to the lower right, groups of heads whispering, consorting. In each case, the layered feel of the images described earlier in this chapter appears to the audience in methodical stages, as if to introduce the viewer to how varying forms of visual style function narratively and thematically. Multiple layers of meaning here deliberately overlap to create ambiguity about different elements that are integral to the story. Here the animators use art technique to endow various layers of thematic meaning in the image, usually refusing to resolve basic questions about the status of the image in the process.

Figure 2.12 Miles' thoughts seem to overwhelm the screen

Conclusion

As the audience experiences these opening passages, watching Miles navigate his Brooklyn home and later Visions Academy, numerous visual and audible elements cue distinct shifts in the graphic texture of the image. Not only that, but rather than resolve the space between the varying styles of the film, these changes incur basic narrative ambiguities about the main character's subjectivity, his relationship to the images depicted on screen, and the status of the film as whole, which functions as a remediated work of art in adapted form. To borrow Genette's term once again, this is a film that seems to want to embrace a quite literal meaning of the 'hyper' in *hypertext*, demanding that the viewer reckon with not only a multifarious visual style, but also with simultaneous layers of meaning and possible entry points in nearly every image. After priming audiences with a citational style and an animation process that open out to these sorts of plural connotations, the first act of the *The Spider-Verse* thus prepares audiences for the more unsettling resonances of future moments in Miles' journey, which use a similarly spasmodic touch to draw on an archive of references (*hypotext*) fraught with the conflicts and obstacles that unfortunately characterize the ordinary experiences of so many teen boys of color.

Notes

1 Readers interested in a more sustained theoretical analysis of the intermingled ways that contemporary cinema draws on comic books are also referred to Dru Jeffries' *Comic Book Film Style*, which draws on Genette's terms to propose an expanded taxonomy to specify six modes of interaction between comic book stylistics and live-action, feature film norms. See Jeffries 2017, pp. 22–51.
2 For a detailed discussion of recent Disney properties and their use of CGI, see Benhamou (2022).
3 Both abstract and evocative, crackle became an ideal visual shorthand for Kirby to give his images energy and mystery – described by comic book artist Jason Latour in a practical video essay as 'light moving or bursting through the darkness' (Latour 2022). Over time, 'Kirby Krackle' (also sometimes called 'Kirby dots') became one of his signature visual styles, imitated by others who used a similar profusion of overlapping, rounded shapes to indicate a sense of enigmatic power or unexplained phenomena. Eventually, 'Krackle' became one of Kirby's characteristic contributions during an illustrious six decades of working for DC and Marvel comics.
4 Spider-Verse tutorials almost became a subgenre unto themselves after the release of the film. For an excellent example of an amateur tutorial for how to make the 'glitch' aesthetic using desktop graphic animation software, see 'Spider-Verse Look Tutorial' (2019).
5 A generation of narrative theorists wrote compellingly about the mechanics of how film narrative denotes different styles of objective and subjective

imagery. While there is no space to indulge such a tangent here, important entries in that literature include different theoretical approaches – from the common sense narrative theory of Bruce Kawin's *Mindscreen: Bergman, Godard and First-Person Film* (1978) to the erudite cognitive theoretical framework of Edward Branigan's *Point of View in the Cinema: A Theory of Narration and Subjectivity in Classic Film* (1982) or the compelling phenomenological suggestiveness of Vivian Sobchack's *The Address of the Eye: A Phenomenology of Film Experience* (1992).

3 Racializing the Spider-Verse
'You gotta choose a side'

In one of the primary promotional posters for *Spider-Man: Into the Spider-Verse* a youthful, costumed character leaps into the air (see the frontispiece image at the beginning of this book). Stretching out a hand as if to reach toward the viewer, the figure is clad in a distinctive black mask with red-rimmed, white eye holes. His limbs are splayed in a lurching, athletic position, suggesting both an adolescent scrawniness and nascent athletic powers, but contrasting with the iconic red-and-blue hero positioned just above him, also apparently in mid-leap. Further in the background are several other characters – one costumed in black and white with a pink-hued hoodie; another resembling some sort of robot; two others less legible on a first pass. The Brooklyn bridge nestles in the distance, just visible against a sun-drenched skyline.

The readable elements of the poster are as plentiful as they are ambivalent. While the hero's human identity remains largely concealed beneath the mask, other details offer traces of various affiliations. Vintage Nike Air Jordans, for instance, trail behind him in what looks like a casual (deliberately untied) fashion statement – 'It's a choice', Miles Morales quips at one point in the film. On the back of his neck, the hood of a red sweatshirt is visible, apparently layered beneath his jacket and the arachnid logoed shirt visible on his chest. For those who know Spider-Man, the bridge might also portend a difference from the story's customary Queens location.

The clothes never make the boy, of course, but they do produce a series of possible connotations of who he might be – and how he differs from the Spider-Man just above his head. There may be no overt reference to skin color here, but the character's fashion choices do suggest an age group and cultural identity. Viewers even vaguely familiar with sneaker culture or clothing trends in the US will recognize his black-white-and-red footwear.[1] Most will also see the Jordans in connection to teenage style trends – even when they do not know

DOI: 10.4324/9781003166962-4

Spike Lee's ad campaign from the late 1980s ('Gotta be the shoes!'), or register their broader symbolic resonance as enduring symbols of style, athletic prowess, and business acumen.[2] For its part, the loose hoodie conveys a similar sense of adolescent fashion, even if some viewers remain oblivious to its other loaded connotations. Perhaps still a banal piece of attire to some, the hooded sweatshirt became a tragic visual symbol in 2012 when another unassuming, hoodie-wearing teenager – Trayvon Martin – perished in Sanford, Florida at the hands of a self-appointed neighborhood vigilante.

That there could even be a potential split in how different audiences might read a poster like this one is also emblematic of how the issue of racial representation dwells potently – but does not dominate – in this film. Various details constellate gradually throughout *The Spider-Verse* – turning this newly ascendant hero into a bundle of 'floating signifiers' of the sort that cultural critic Stuart Hall (1997) theorized nearly three decades ago. It is as if any knowledge of recent racial strife in America occupies another significant hypertextual layer of *The Spider-Verse* – perhaps the most consequential of them all. And when the film builds on the legacy of Spider-Man comic books and media, it also intervenes in more recent efforts to racialize the genre of super-hero fiction, thematizing how those revisionist, restorative efforts intertwine in their own swirl of citational energies. In a recent analysis of these dynamics, Isabel Molina-Guzman expresses skepticism about the way that *The Spider-Verse* uses 'color-blind writing and casting' to commercialize mixed-race identity. And yet, she argues, the film also fosters 'an interpretive space for audiences to feel and read race' – a dynamic she enumerates through a review of the numerous celebratory critical and fan responses to it (Molina-Guzmán 2021: 221–2).

While it is clear that *The Spider-Verse* does downplay Miles Morales' ethnic identity as part of its 'universalist' appeal, this chapter seeks to account more fully for how it nevertheless allows for what Molina-Guzmán calls 'interpretive space'. In this way, the analysis attempted here is not unlike the one Maria Flood offers in her compelling book on *Moonlight* (Barry Jenkins, 2016), another film in the 'Cinema and Youth Cultures' series that navigates the precarious ground between the universal and particular resonances of a coming-of-age story about a young boy of color (Flood 2021). Drawing on the work of bell hooks and Sara Ahmed, among others, Flood opines that while she cannot approximate the looks or experiences of the diverse cultures represented in the film, it is the 'encounters between visual cultures, their makers, viewers and interpreters' that comprise 'the productive spaces that make art compelling, vibrant, urgent and necessary' (2021: 3).

This section of the book works to highlight further how *The Spider-Verse* creates the potential for the 'productive spaces' that Flood describes. Past chapters have described how *The Spider-Verse* uses various techniques to refer to the archive of previous Spider-Men – what they have termed the *hypotext* – behind its iconic character and his origin story. That creative work centers on Miles and his story, conveyed through the film's organizing metaphor – the multiverse – which at first seems to suggest limitless, creative expansiveness. But beyond structural analysis, the film also quickly lets the audience know that going 'into' the Spider-Verse also means reckoning with forms of equity and inclusion. Though these dynamics are rarely conveyed directly by the film's dramatic arc or dialogue, they arrive nevertheless at some of the film's most poignant moments, surfacing in a subtle combination of visual and sonic elements that suggest the challenges that boys of color face in contemporary American culture.

Afro-Latino Boyhood and Spider-Man

Miles Morales' multiracial identity has been a constant, if unevenly developed, part of his character since his debut in *Ultimate Fallout* #4 in 2011. That unevenness begins with the character's name. Despite the pleasing alliteration of 'Miles' and 'Morales', many early readers of the comics pointed out that this son of a Black man and a Puerto Rican woman would not generally be likely to take his mother's last name, at least in an American context. Given the representational purposes of the initial run of comics, the pairing of his names led to several popular hypotheses among the fan base, including the possibility that his mother wanted to maintain the Hispanic tradition of placing the maternal name last in a sequence (in which case Miles' second name would become 'Davis'), or that his father may have wished to avoid an obvious callback to another iconic African-American pairing – 'Miles Davis'. Despite rampant speculation along these lines, the reasons for his last name were never addressed directly in either the comics or in Reynolds' novelization of them. Later, the issue was apparently resolved in a series from 2016 – where Jefferson explains to his son that he changed the name to avoid association with his younger brother's ongoing criminal disrepute. Still, that explanation overlooks yet another possible symbolic wrinkle in the name combination – since Miles' father also happens to bear the moniker of one of the most infamous leaders of the Confederate South.

Loaded games of symbolic interpretation, of course, are part and parcel of the current American climate of racial protest. Present reckons with past in fits and starts, and iconic elements circulate in meme culture, appropriated and reappropriated by different groups for different ends. As this book is written, revisionist accounts like *The 1619 Project* continue to win widespread acclaim for re-reading the nation's history in light of slavery.[3] And as they continue to also generate backlash from conservative activists, a new ground game in the current version of an age-old battle now takes place online. In this context, Miles' hoodie might be the least overt – yet most recognizable – part of the poster analyzed above. Beginning in 2012, largely in response to Trayvon Martin's death, a response to law enforcement's frequent, unthinkable crimes against Black citizens gradually coalesced on Twitter, eventually forming a decentered movement – Black Lives Matter – which continues to foment a powerful new protest strategy to this day. As Martin's assailant somehow escaped conviction, thousands of protesters showed up around the nation for 'hoodie marches' to express both the banal and universal presence of the victim's chosen attire, so common among Black youth – and youth in general. Simultaneously, many Black celebrities uploaded 'hoodie selfies' in a Twitter campaign to express their solidarity with the Martin family, including NBA star LeBron James and his Miami Heat teammates. Eventually, President Barack Obama lamented that 'if [he] had a son, he would look like Trayvon' (quoted in Demby 2012).

As the deaths of other unarmed citizens seem to continue unabated – George Floyd, Tamir Rice, Michael Brown, Ahmaud Arbury, Philando Castille, Freddie Gray, Breonna Taylor – striated black-and-white 'Black Lives Matter' signs reappear periodically in the streets, in front yards, and on social media accounts. Tragically, the decade since Martin and the emergence of BLM has also been defined by reactionary responses to these pleas for visibility – from 'All Lives Matter' chants by predominantly white counter-protesters, to 'Back the Blue' pro-police yard signs, and most insidious of all, the insurgent political campaign of Donald J. Trump, who in the latter half of Obama's presidency channeled racist sentiments by espousing a racist 'birther' conspiracy about Obama's citizenship and ethnic origins into a legion of Twitter followers, eventually riding that momentum to the presidency in 2016, the insurrection of January 6, 2020, and an uncertain political beyond.[4]

Over the past decade, academic responses to these events have led to calls for increased focus on Black and brown masculinity studies. Writing partly in response to the tragic deaths of Rice and Martin, among so many others, co-authors Michael J. Dumas and Joseph Derrick Nelson voiced the cries of BLM activists in scholarly terms with an article published two years before *The Spider-Verse* was released. 'Black boyhood itself', they write, 'has been rendered both unimagined and unimaginable due to the inability of American society – and especially law enforcement – to see them as children rather than immanent threats to the social order' (Dumas and Nelson 2016: 28). As other recent scholarship on the depiction of Black boyhood demonstrates, it is not at all clear that the current American media industries, despite growing awareness of the need, have offered any real answers to this problem. In a poignant call for more politically-informed readings of how Black men have been policed – both literally and figuratively – across a gamut of putatively 'liberal' films and television series of the early 21st century, Jared Sexton asks, 'What, if anything, can be done with [Black men and boys], given what has been done to them, that is, given their structural disinheritance?' (2017: xii–xiii). Though he studiously avoids simple answers to this question, Sexton's readings of films like *Training Day* (Antoine Fuqua, 2008) and *The Blind Side* (John Lee Hancock, 2009) demonstrate that recent depictions of Black men and boys, whatever their noble intentions, often end by perpetuating what he calls 'antiblack black visibility' (xxiii).

Similar structural challenges pervade the efforts of film historians seeking ways to narrativize how Black cinema has developed in America since the end of Civil Rights. All share in the challenge of celebrating progress while properly accounting for ongoing systemic racism in an industry where white privilege continues to overdetermine casting and undergird funding. In his pioneering critical history of Black cinema in America, Ed Guerrero reflects on the impossibility of conceptualizing his topic without a dream that Black filmmaking will somehow, someday reach the status of a more universal image – and that his book will one day be received both as 'a *black* document' and one that affirms Black people to find 'their full potential and humanity on the big screen, *universal* in all their soundings, rhythms, resistances, and signifying illuminations' (Guerrero 1993: 7, emphasis in original).

In his industrially informed study of Black cinema in the US, Mark Reid highlights the inequity of economic ownership, separating feature films that are truly 'independent' (Black-owned and operated) from 'commercial' (white controlled) ones, and factors these material considerations into his readings of thematic elements (Reid 1993: 1–4). While granting the relevance of economic factors of production, recent scholars of race also tend to resist such categorical distinctions in the name of a more mobile form of criticism that weighs different factors without *a priori* judgements of their potential for aesthetic interest. Michael Boyce Gillespie, for instance, rejects any one pragmatic definition of Black film in favor of a targeted mode of criticism that 'persistently wrestles with the question of identity as something other than a fixed signifier' (2016: 7).

It is in the vein of Gillespie's formulation that the current account proposes to understand how *The Spider-Verse* approaches racial representation. For throughout *The Spider-Verse* and its promotional materials, we find a 'persistent wrestling' with modes of representation and their consequences for mainstream filmmaking. In an interview during the lead-up to the 2019 Oscars, filmmaker Ava DuVernay praised the racial representation in the film, while also acknowledging its subtlety. At the end of an in-depth discussion with the film's directorial trio, she pressed for details on the characterization of Miles Morales. To what extent, she asked, did the racial heritage of this Afro-Latino teenager – chosen to replace an iconic white character – make a difference to their creative process? Or, as DuVernay put it, did they simply just create the same type of character and 'color him brown?' (DuVernay 2019).

The ensuing exchange is revealing. In his initial response, Perischetti insisted that one of their creative goals was to make Miles and his cultural background – his multiracial identity – 'the very core' of his depiction on screen. He claimed that this notion was present for the creative team 'from the ground up', and that they valued authenticity so much that they began conceiving the character with on-location research into the day-to-day experiences of the Brooklyn school system (Perischetti, quoted in DuVernay 2019). His colleague, Ramsey, the lone Black director of the three, followed up these comments with a quick but telling qualification – that their goal was to 'understand Miles as a person' but that this would also be the case for 'any character' they created (Ramsey, quoted in DuVernay 2019).

There is a certain familiar irony here about the unspoken parameters of racialized discourse in popular culture. DuVernay nods vigorously in agreement at the directors' responses, highlighting how for the two Black creatives involved in the interview, communicating sensitive ideas like these means navigating *how* to speak about race in a public forum. For Ramsey, accessing the authenticity of Miles means treating him like 'any other' character. What he does not say, of course, is that in Hollywood, 'any character' has usually been white. Meanwhile, Afro-Latino boys have almost never even been *a* character, let alone the *main* character of a superhero film. This rhetorical tightrope walk continued on social media as the film gained in prominence. DuVernay publicly advocated for *The Spider-Verse*'s Academy Award campaign after the nominations were announced, and when it eventually won, she tweeted a quote from the film to Ramsey and the other directors, including a cover of Miles Morales from *Ultimate Comics*. Unattributed at the top of the tweet are the dying words of Miles' Uncle Aaron (voiced by Mahershala Ali in the film): 'You're the best of us, Miles. You're on your way. Just keep going.'

In some ways, the lack of explicit context in the tweet allows implications to float more freely – leaving it to various online communities to read the words, chime in, fill in the gaps. Those who 'hear' the racialized implications of Aaron's quote and connect them to the film can thus follow the meaning, whereas others do not. This was true of many of the retweets of DuVernay's post, as well as for the co-hosts of *The Wrap*'s 'Low Key' podcast, who reviewed *The Spider-Verse* shortly after its release and spent an entire episode summarizing all the ways that they 'heard' racialized content in the film even without explicit reference points. As co-host Aaron Lanton put it, 'There is so much Black cinema where they say "the best of us", like "you're the best of us". I was like, "They snuck that in there, but we heard it! No one else heard it, but Black viewers did!"' (quoted in Molloy 2018).

These public exchanges about *The Spider-Verse* also rhyme with how the film participates in discourses of race more generally. Producing a mainstream animated film for families, the film's creators were deliberate about maintaining a story coated with a 'universal' veneer. And yet, numerous moments of screen time also resonate with a racialized subtext, often made possible by the dynamics that exist between the layers of citation and animation already covered in this book (see Chapters 1 and 2). The film's workflow, variously described as 'chaotic' and 'collaborative' by its participants, managed to fly largely under the radar at Sony Pictures Animation, and in the process accumulated numerous authentic notes from the cast and crew. These included the experienced leadership of Ramsey, but also the vocal performances of the principal actors – Shameik Moore (Miles), Brian Tyree Henry (Jefferson) and Ali (Aaron) – whose improvised inflections on their delivery of lines would frequently inspire the animators to return once again to rethink sequences and add nuance to how the characters interacted (DuVernay 2019). In many cases, the film combines hypertextual features of image and sound to present the audience with a jumble of suggestive elements at once, thematizing Miles' growth as a person, his development as Spider-Man, and his experience as a young person of color integrating a canonized narrative universe long dominated by whiteness.

No Expectations

Though Miles Morales' arrival in the comics was generally well received at the time, the details of his story have in some cases not aged well. Notably, while Bendis and Pichelli's initial comics versions of the character found some success as a new Spider-Man, complete with a new suit and different superpowers, he never really managed to shed his secondary status to Parker's original version of the character. The second issue of *Ultimate Fallout* confronts this dynamic obliquely; Miles first fights crime in his Spider-suit after Peter's death and hears criticism from Brooklyn citizens who claim that his reappropriation of the attire is 'in bad taste'. In a later run of the comics, Miles' problematic position as an alternative to Peter Parker rather than the unquestioned star of his own story gets thematized in more thorough ways, none clearer than a moment in *Spider-Man* #2 (2016). After Miles' identity is accidentally revealed, his friend Ganke points out the excited response of a white female vlogger to the revelation of a Black Spider-Man. Miles responds negatively to her 'qualification' of his race behind the heroic name – 'I don't want to be a Black Spider-Man', he says, 'I want to be Spider-Man'.

The emotions expressed by Bendis via Miles here are complicated to read, especially when coming from the mind of a white writer. Lively Twitter debates about the issue ensued, revealing a fan base attuned to the essential philosophical question of representation reproduced in these panels – i.e., whether to be recognized as a universal hero (Spider-Man) means having to eschew a particular cultural identity (Black). For instance, Omar Holmon, a prominent comics blogger and critic for the website *Black Nerd Problems,* first wrote a glowing review of *Spider-Man* #2, focusing on its rare engagement with race. In a first pass, Holmon lauded Bendis for the courage to broach the topic: 'I didn't think we'd be seeing Miles take on being a dark-skinned Spider-Man at all' (Holmon no date a). A few days later though, Holmon walked back on his praise, apparently in light of numerous conversations with his peers:

> Miles saying I don't want to be Black Spider-man I just want to Spider-Man is like President Barack Obama proclaiming: I don't want to be The 'First Black' President I just want to be The President. Hashtag never going to go down that way. With this response Bendis not only undermines the real need and desire for representation, he also just straight up acts like race is unimportant/irrelevant.
>
> (Holmon no date b)

Holmon's commentary here is consistent with recent academic responses to Miles as he appears in the Bendis/Pichelli comics. In their consideration of Marvel's recent reworkings of several iconic characters in the comics, Monica Flegel and Judith Leggatt argue that, despite a clear potential for ground-breaking representation, Miles Morales and Kamala Khan (a Pakistani teen girl who replaces Ms. Marvel in another popular series) ultimately do little to trouble the *status quo* of white supremacy in comics. This is because the characters are relatable in a way that '[fits] into the cultural tapestry without challenging it' (Flegel and Leggatt 2021: 57). In the comic versions of these characters, the co-authors argue, maintaining the possibility of simultaneous universal and specific readings means that audiences of color may read the films as inclusive of their experiences, but that white audiences can also proceed with the assumption that these new characters are meant as mere variations on a white norm, since their stories treat their 'ethnicity as surface performance' that is peripheral to the main story and heroics (87). In an intricate analysis of what he also calls the 'color-blind' politics of the film, Dru Jeffries argues that the multifaceted stylistic features of the film analyzed in Chapter 2 actually support that mandate, effectively working to minimize Miles' significance within the franchise – and reinforce the animated film's secondary status to Tom Holland's concurrent adventures in the MCU film *Spider-Man: Homecoming* (Jeffries 2022: 206). Along similar lines, Sam Summers argues that the design of the film evinces a problematic ahistoricism – evoking nostalgia for 'older' versions of comic book art without confronting how those same cherished panels of the past never troubled themselves with the kinds of diversity that Miles and his friends seek to represent (Summers 2019: 190–94).

For other critics around the time of its release, *The Spider-Verse* seemed to gain at least some progressive ground over these earlier representations of Miles. In his book length study of racial representation in Marvel more generally, Jeffrey A. Brown broadly agrees with critics that the first Black Spider-Man's comic origins were frustratingly limited, but also argues that *The Spider-Verse* as a film pushes beyond this type of depiction, centering Miles as a character in a way that makes his experiences more legible as universal rather than a mere variation on a white default (Brown 2021: 18). To Brown's point, it is useful to show how the hypertextual elements of the film's animation (see Chapter 2) also become a key to unlocking some of the most ambivalent moments where the audience must reckon with (rather than brush aside) the flux of different representations in the multiverse.

Here considering previous Miles Morales adventures is also relevant to discussing the creative choices taken in the film. The movie nods to its creative debts to both the *Ultimate Fallout* storyline, written for Marvel comics by Bendis, and the plot of Jason Reynolds' young adult novel, *Miles Morales: Spider-Man* (2017). Notably, in one scene three extra names – Reynolds, Bendis, and *Fallout* illustrator Sara Pichelli – appear as contacts on Miles' cell phone registry while he checks for a message from Uncle Aaron. In Reynolds, the creative team invokes the influence of a writer who also rewrote Ibrahim Xendi's *Stamped from the Beginning: The Definitive History of Racist Ideas in America* (2016) for youth readers. In all three versions – the comic, Reynolds' novel, and the film – Brooklyn Visions Academy is key to the main conflict of the story, with significant differences in emphasis. In Bendis and Pichelli's comic version, the role of the school itself is minimized, but it does become symbolic of Miles' experience of systemic inequity; Miles feels out of place at the school, and his only authentic contact there is his friend Ganke. For the novelization of Miles' story, Reynolds freely interpreted the school, turning it into the main device for conflict in a revisionist account that 'actively works to dismantle racial hierarchies' by questioning how educational institutions reinforce canonical forms of white supremacy (Worlds and Miller, 2019: 46). The primary antagonist is Mr. Chamberlain, an elderly white teacher whose villainy takes the form of gaslighting through a faux-Socratic form of 'questioning' the facts of American history. As Reynolds says, 'I tried to take a huge issue in America and personify it as an old man' (quoted in Richards 2017).

In his sessions, Chamberlain lectures from a performed position of 'objectivity', arguing that US history might have an alternative reading of the Civil War wherein the South was persecuted for slavery by a hypocritical North that was equally dependent on slave labor. Later, the students in the classroom take issue with this depiction, led by Miles' crush, a poet named Julia. When students are suspended for their actions, Miles follows Chamberlain after school, discovering that the old teacher is part of a secret society connected to the local prison and a shadowy character called 'The Warden'. Through the Chamberlain-Warden axis of evil in his story, Reynolds dramatizes how conservative discourses of 'free speech' in the classroom relate to institutionalized powers maintaining white privilege – here by depicting a fictionalized (and quite literal) rendition of the 'school to prison' pipeline between Brooklyn Visions and the prison system (Worlds and Miller 2019: 44).

In any case, scenes in the classroom in *The Spider-Verse* are far less frequent than they are in Reynolds' novel, where educational spaces make up a primary location for the action. As Dru Jeffries points out in his lengthy critique of the film, *The Spider-Verse* configures Brooklyn Visions as a product of affirmative action policy, but never really engages with its consequences overtly (Jeffries 2022, 202–03). In the Bendis-Pichelli original, Miles wins a seat at the prestigious crosstown school by dint of an educational lottery – backstory that receives an extended scene in the pages of *Ultimate Fallout*. However, in the updated screen rendition, that crucial contextual information is reduced to a split second – when a blue ball emblazoned with '42' flashes by with no explanation in the film's opening montage. Like innumerable other references in the film, the moment happens so quickly that viewers unacquainted with the Bendis version might not even recognize its relation to the school. Some could explain the number as an (equally pertinent) homage to Jackie Robinson's jersey number, but some might also ignore it completely. This potential split of readings, for Jeffries, suggests a film where important features are continually 'downplayed' in apparent acquiescence to a risk-averse mainstream politics of representation (Jeffries 2022, 202).

And yet, the connections between pedagogy and systemic inequity are also treated more compellingly in other portions of the film, at least for those who care to look. Just seven minutes in, during a rapid-fire, thirty-second montage sequence that encapsulates the stress of his day at school, we see that Miles is studying *Great Expectations*. An early nod to Dickens in the first act of *The Spider-Verse* seems reasonable, since learning about the conventions of the *bildungsroman* would make sense for the curriculum at Visions. In the Dickens novel, Phillip 'Pip' Pirrip is an orphan who must overcome his impoverished background to gain more respectability and, eventually, win the heart of Estella, his childhood love. The first mention of *Great Expectations* arises in a series of snippets of classroom scenes with a cacophony of teachers shouting out various concepts or assignments. The montage may first read as a summative statement about our hero's disorientation in a new school.

As with most other sequences of *The Spider-Verse*, a rewatch rewards with other significant details. Just prior to a shot of the balding, bespectacled teacher who brandishes a volume of the Dickens novel, we see Miles in another classroom, apparently learning the basic rules of logical deduction. The teacher here is white and female, and we just hear a few choice words – 'it's a syllogism' – during a split-second where we also see the backs of her pupils' heads (see Figure 3.1).

Figure 3.1 Students learn about syllogisms at Visions Academy

Buried in the connotative dimensions of this image, *The Spider-Verse* constellates numerous reading positions on the logic of inclusion. On the one hand, the scene playfully refers to a well-known moment in the teaching of logical reasoning, which includes a premise ('All men are mortal'), a minor premise ('Socrates is a man'), and a logical conclusion ('Therefore, Socrates is mortal'). At the same time, the scene also gestures at several notable possible exceptions to that rule. Not a mistake, for instance, that Wanda/Gwen's hair is just below the words 'all men', as if to point out the gendered bias of this classical reasoning lesson. Meanwhile, Miles, whose hairstyle is by now recognizable and staged center-screen, blocks out a conspicuous word in the deduction – 'man' – with a recognizable detail of ethnic difference.

Miles is many things – a boy, a teenager, a soon-to-be mutant, a future superhero – but none of them fits the word we associate with the Socrates syllogism that the teacher is presenting to her class. Within this purportedly 'relatable' depiction of a classroom experience in a teen film, similar to so many others from *Ferris Bueller's Day Off* (Hughes, 1986) to *Mean Girls* (Waters, 2004), *The Spider-Verse* also gestures at how the normative rhetoric of classroom education bears the potential to exclude. An oblique reference to the end of Spike Lee's *Malcolm X* (1992) could also be in the offing here, as in the cameo of Nelson Mandela, who quotes Malcolm in a classroom, proclaiming "I am a man". In any case, Miles does not want to be at Brooklyn Visions; we have just seen him resist going there in the previous scene where his father drops him off that morning. He later self-sabotages his results on a Physics quiz, prompting his teacher to assign him an extra essay which is 'not about physics, but about you and what kind of person you want to be'. Cut to Miles later that night, behind his desk at home, surrounded with books, beginning to write his essay on a legal pad. The page is yellow and blank other than the words 'Great Expectations' at the top. Still struggling to fulfill the assignment he sneaks out of his bedroom window to visit his Uncle Aaron. Once at his uncle's apartment, he reveals another concept he has been working up in his sketchbook, this one visual and colorful.

Only later, in the subway, is the audience aware that the same design – a vivid jumble of colorful lines – will be what Miles affixes to the subway wall alongside his uncle later that night. In that scene, Miles sprays his creative vision on the wall, listening to another vintage hip hop tune (Black Sheep's 'The Choice is Yours') where the lyrics ('You can get with this, or you can get with that') seem to thematize the distinctions between what he is doing now and what we just watched him do in the previous scene. In the subterranean Brooklyn of the night, Uncle Aaron helps his nephew add the final touch, affixing a white line around Miles' body in a vertical orientation that disrupts the words 'No Expectations' behind it, but also bears an eerie resemblance to the outline of a corpse at a crime scene (see Figure 3.2). 'I see just what you are getting at', Aaron tells his nephew. Before they leave, Miles pauses to take a picture with his cell phone; an oddly gleaming spider lands on his hand (see Chapter 2).

It is with subtle details like these that *The Spider-Verse* manages to evoke the racial connotations of Miles' story without explicitly doing so. Having Miles express his misgivings in graffiti rather than written form not only contextualizes his creative potential as a character, but also grants an ambiguity to the sentiments he is expressing. Though his identity as the Prowler has not yet been revealed, Uncle Aaron – an underground artist who listens to Biggie Smalls – has already been coded as the foil to his estranged brother, a PDNY cop who shares his name with the Confederate President. Much as Miles' hair obscures the word 'man' on the teacher's chalkboard demonstration, the film

Figure 3.2 Aaron helps his nephew add the final touch to his artwork

advances sentiments of racial exclusion and oppression gradually, using various techniques to highlight unstated comparisons that float in the various dimensions of the image and soundtrack. Once they are apparent, though, it becomes difficult not to see how ideas about racial representation underlie many of the visual and audible textures of the rest of the film.

Miles vs the Enthymeme

Much as Ramsey and DuVernay carefully choose their rhetoric in the interview cited above, the opening passages of the film never nakedly proclaim the racial dimensions of Miles' experience. A strength of *The Spider-Verse*, as mentioned in previous chapters, lies in its embrace of a hypertextual style – one that multiplies Easter Eggs and possible 'entryways' at an almost dizzying pace. What this means is that the references to *Great Expectations* and classical logic teaching mentioned in the previous section fly by so quickly in the film's first act that viewers might not even notice them. Plausible deniability exists, then, for those who want to look past the racialized subtext, for instance, of the spray paint outline of Miles' graffiti creation – especially when combined with the words 'No Expectations'. Miles could just be expressing narrow frustration at the universal experience of a teenager unable to capitulate to the high standards of a new teacher. Yet as the subsequent passage with Uncle Aaron suggests, that frustration is also a matter of how Miles is *seen* by those teachers, and of how their lessons connect (or do not connect) to his authentic experience as a multiracial teenager.

As other opening sequences of the film flit by, the second, more provocative of these two readings is repeatedly – if rapidly – communicated to those who want to see it. For one thing, Miles' humor and relatability as a youth character often have to do with how he jokingly points out the hidden premises of collective logic. This trait is consistent with Peter Parker in all his previous incarnations, of course, but the moments for Miles somehow always have something extra. In the previous scene that shows his late arrival to Physics class, for instance, Miles pokes fun at his teacher by citing Einstein, asking whether perhaps he is not late – but rather everyone else is early. Here a joke exposes the ideological grounding of the situation at hand. The traditional logic of the teacher would read that 'all students who are on time are already present' and 'Miles is not already present'. Therefore, the buried premise that must be accepted to reach the collective conclusion ('Miles is not on time') would be that 'time is a constant'. As many audience members will recognize – and as

Wanda/Gwen signals by snickering – this fleeting joke has profound possible implications. Notably, that there might be a world where time is *not* a constant, like the one with multiple dimensions that they (and the audience) are about to enter shortly.

Playful invocations of Socrates and Einstein thus serve not only to establish the instructional climate at Brooklyn Visions Academy, but also to encourage viewers to think critically about the act of logical deduction and its relationship to a 'high achievement' school culture – and to a film about revisionist representation. Whereas the shot of the classroom pokes holes in the exclusionary language of syllogisms by foregrounding the shapes of Gwen (a white teen girl) and Miles (a multiracial teen boy), the scene in Physics reminds us of how Einstein's theory of relativity unseats one of science's most famous assumptions about time as a constant. In deductive terms, both these examples could be referred to as enthymemes, or unstated assumptions that cement logical deductions. Scholars of rhetoric and linguistics have written at more length about how enthymemic logic frequently sustains dominant ideology by remaining unspoken, therefore unquestioned (Jackson 2006; Houdek 2018). These can sometimes include damaging misperceptions about ethnic groups or cultures that are perpetuated over time.

In his introduction to Reynolds' adaptation of his book, Xendi sketches the deductive differences between three predominant views of race in America, two racist and one antiracist. Segregationists and assimilationists, he writes, while they differ on the solutions, both 'think there is something wrong with Black people and that's why Black people are on the lower and dying end of racial inequity'. Antiracists instead push back against these views by asserting that 'there is nothing wrong or right about Black people and everything wrong with *racism*' (Xendi 2020: 6). In deductive logic, the difference between these views is termed one of enthymemic reasoning, which derives conclusions from hidden larger premises. In the first two variations – segregationist and assimilationist – the plight of Black and brown people is caused by something wrong with them, whereas in the antiracist deduction that logic is replaced by a systemic view. In other words, antiracist logic replaces the racist tendency of one unstated premise ('inequity exists because there is something wrong with Black people') with a new one that shifts the ground to systemic conditions ('inequity exists because there is something wrong with society'). Cast against this more self-aware backdrop, it becomes clear that Miles' Physics teacher may also have misdiagnosed the source of her student's self-sabotage, assuming that it is because of him rather than because of the ways he fails to connect with the curriculum at his new school. In other words, rather than making his failure a question of 'what kind of person [he wants] to be', she could have asked instead what systemic problems persist at Visions – an elite school with great expectations – after they admit a student of color.

These moments would be far less interesting if they remained in such a primary form. But of course, logical deductions are not always straightforward for a film. This is, after all, also a superhero film, a genre where bodily exploits become a spectacle, and hence where conventional tropes can provide their own form of deductive reasoning. As *The Spider-Verse* unfolds, other scenes offer moments where Miles is presented in physical situations that suggest similar deductive choices, as if to offer a high stakes game of separating the potential consequences of racial representation on-screen. One of these moments arguably occurs right after Miles jokes about Einstein. For as he speaks, his face is also conspicuously washed out by the light of the classroom projection (see Figure 3.3).

As the video of Dr. Liv Octavius speaks over his words in the documentary about parallel dimensions, it becomes clear that many of the other students in the classroom are not even listening to his jovial excuses. In an interview about the sequel to *Miles Morales: Spider-Man*, Reynolds identifies his essential approach to racializing the experiences of his main character. He asks, 'what does it mean to put on a mask and be invisible and then take off the mask and still be invisible?' (quoted in Belt 2023). As Miles' apparent attempts to fit in are undercut by the bright light that renders his body hard to see, it becomes challenging to imagine a more fitting visual rendering of this idea.

The projection scene, too, helps introduce the audience to 'G …Wanda' (Hailee Stanfield), the lone classmate who responds to Miles' temporal joke. The two engage in an awkward exchange, whispering covertly in the

Figure 3.3 Miles' face is washed out by a classroom projection

darkness in an interaction that strongly suggests 'meet cute' potential for our hero – at least for those viewers who respond to conventional teen comedy or rom com cues. On numerous other levels though, the interaction is far from neutral. Scenes later, 'Wanda' will later be revealed to actually be Gwen Stacy / Spider-Gwen, swinging into an action scene in the nick of time to save Miles and Peter B. Parker from the clutches of Octavius as they flee from Alchemax. Even as a mere civilian character, Stacy carries more than her fair share of hypotextual baggage in Spider-Man franchise history. At one point, the character was most notable to comic fans for her tragic death in *The Amazing Spider-Man* #121 (1972) – entitled 'The Night Gwen Stacy Died' – a scenario reprised memorably by Emma Stone and Andrew Garfield in *The Amazing Spider-Man* 2 (Marc Webb, 2014). After decades of accumulated fan interest and sympathy, often bemoaning her untimely fate, Stacy was then brought back as a masked hero in her own right, recreated as Spider-Gwen by Jason Latour and Robbi Rodriguez for Earth-65, an alternate universe in another Marvel timeline from *Edge of Spider-Verse* #2 (2014), itself an offshoot of Dan Slott's successful *Amazing Spider-Man* storyline (Ching 2015).

Sadly, there are other immanent readings of Miles and Gwen that are even more tragic than the comics version that some 'knowing' audience members will register. Much like the loaded connotations of the uncle-son scenes enumerated above, a racialized reading of *The Spider-Verse* must also acknowledge the specter of historical violence lurking just behind any suggestion of coupling between these two characters. And anyone acquainted with the historical dangers of interracial comingling in America knows that Hollywood romantic conventions – a flirty 'meet cute' with a white girl – could have had dire consequences for someone who looked like Miles – especially in the 1960s or earlier. After all, Peter Parker's comics debut occurred just seven years after the death of Emmet Till. Without spoilers, it is safe to say that Gwen's symbolic duplicity in this regard also extends to the film's sequels, where her role as Miles' ally (in several senses of the word) comes increasingly into conflict with her status as a female, white Spider-Person.

Racialized Dimensions

Numerous other scenes of the film seem constructed to present similar visual and sonic analogies for the plight of a character whose story arc embodies the identarian paradox – and possible danger – of bringing a 'diverse' Spider-Man to the screen. In so doing, they often ask the viewer to weigh the universal elements of the Spider-Man story against the particularized ways that Miles' appearance and experience differ from the norm. Previous iterations of Peter Parker already included adolescent awkwardness and social exclusion, and this new Afro-Latino edition of the superhero is, in many ways, no different. On the other hand, as we have seen, the film also casts Miles' adventures amidst a flux of signifiers that reference his 'otherness' from the canon. In other words, if the first act of the film establishes this type of layered awareness against a backdrop of familiar scenes from high school and the teen comedy genre, later sequences play with a higher stakes game of identification, provocatively presenting us with images that reckon with racial violence.

As discussed in Chapter 1, Peter Parker (Chris Pine) is given the first word in the film, introducing the viewer to both the film and the exceptional ways in which it will be interacting with usual audience expectations for Spider-Man's origin story ('Let's do this one last time'). In the scene just following his spider bite, Miles' emerging Spider-sense takes him to the scene of a battle between the Kingpin (Liev Schreiber) and his various minions – including an enormous, flying rendition of the Green Goblin. Though the hero first addresses Miles with cocksure confidence, he is soon overwhelmed by the force of the Goblin and another villain – the purple clad Prowler. The Super Collider, it turns out, occupies a hinge point between not only spatial dimensions, but also for the graphic distinctions between comics and film. Both fractally divided image 'glitches' and a stream of explosive 'Kirby Krackle' testify to a frenzied multimedia aspect to these affairs (see Chapter 2). Spider-Man must fight the Goblin and Prowler, and in a series of blows, he is thrown into the path of the Super Collider's laser flow just as it splices dimensions. Miles manages to speak with Peter as he lies prostrate in the rubble – joking that all will be fine, clearly unable to move. He then gives Miles a flash drive needed to disarm the dastardly time machine. Miles hides behind some debris just as the Kingpin arrives, unmasking this Brooklyn's Parker (he is blonde!) before shooting and killing him in cold blood.

All these events set the stage in various ways for the arrival of Miles' second encounter with Spider-Man's own canonized whiteness. The Kingpin, for his part, makes whiteness into both literally and figuratively larger than life villainy. Though he is ostensibly a flesh-and-blood human character – like Miles, Gwen, Peter, and other scenic 'extras' in Brooklyn – he also stands in contrast to them in terms of art style. Previous comic versions of the character depict him as stocky and quite large, but this version looks ripped from another graphic dimension entirely, drawn with angular, hulking shoulders and moving on the screen like a dark shape blotting out the colors around him, with a round head hunched into his chest. These visual elements are redoubled by Schreiber's clipped, gruff vocal performance – perhaps channeling his television role on *Ray Donovan* (Showtime, 2013–20) – and the spasmodic sounds of his revolver, which claps loudly and flatly with no reverb on the soundtrack, as if to reject the sonic dimensionality of the space, then to kill his victims with echoless, ominous finality. There is a backstory for his motives – he regrets the deaths of his wife and child in a train accident and wrongly blames Spider-Man for them. And yet, his terse, merciless comportment also offers scant space for sympathy. In all these characteristics, the Kingpin also provides a convenient foil for the other white characters, and in particular for the derelict, overweight version of Parker who arrives a few scenes later.[5] Against a backdrop of expressionistic gangsterism, Peter B. gains latitude to be a comedic, less-offensive role model for our impressionable hero. He may be slovenly and crass, but his version of white mediocrity pales by comparison with the Kingpin's outright criminal malevolence.

Miles retreats to the Brooklyn surface after the explosion, overwhelmed by his fast-encroaching Spider powers and his assigned duty – a dead superhero's last hope to disable the Super Collider. He heads to a costume shop to find a Spider suit, managing on his boarding school budget only to purchase an ill-fitting Halloween version from a gleefully winking merchant (also a Stan Lee cameo for diehard fans). The confluence of superpowers and mise-en-scène here also provides the filmmakers with an opportunity to play on the boundaries of racial representation in the crosshairs of media translation. Miles ventures to Parker's gravesite at night, and another shadowy figure approaches him from behind. In a jump scare the audience shares, Miles deploys a burst of fluid from his wrist, not entirely in control of his new web spinning powers. A tall figure is knocked unconscious against the wall of an adjacent church, and Miles approaches him, asking 'Who are you?' What follows is a remarkable montage of possible meaning. As if in response, the frame of the screen devolves into the frames of a comic book, its pages flipping as if to conjoin the audience's perspective with Miles' efforts to place this episode in his own knowledge of Spider-Man canon; the most prominent frame features Spider-Man asking 'Who are you?' along with other frames that appear to be set in the same snowy graveyard milieu as the scene currently playing out.

Abruptly, a voice-over narration returns as if in response to the question, bringing back a familiar phrase ('Okay, let's do this one last time …'). This time, however, we see a different name on the name tag – Peter B. Parker – this time voiced by Jake Johnson in slightly more phlegmatic tones than Pine. In evidence of the film's narrative compactness, this montage also explains the mechanics of the multi-verse collapse, showing how Peter B. – a paunchy, thirty-something iteration of the character – got yanked out of an ordinary evening of eating pizza into a blizzard of glitchy, Kirby Krackling visual grandeur, only to be dropped unceremoniously into Miles' Brooklyn. Cut back to the filmic present, where Miles attempts to awaken this new Peter, only to be threatened by the whooping sound of sirens, the flood of a flashlight, and a threatening voice 'Get your hands up!' What follows is a split-second, signature moment, as Miles thrusts Peter B.'s semi-con-scious torso against the wall, propping his visibly white palms back with his own (visibly brown) ones, and wedging his chin back below a terrified, masked face (see Figure 3.4).

Much like the earlier scenes at Visions Academy, the interpretive potential here seems loaded to express not only Miles' frantic reac-tions, but also the symbolic plight of the hero as a character. Doubt-less, any replacement Spider-Man, tasked with replacing Peter and deactivating the Super Collider, would experience an awkward inter-action with the authorities here. Moreover, Miles' fear could be seen as purely circumstantial – he knows he is dressed as Spider-Man, that Peter is unconscious, and that law enforcement (like his own father) is disinclined to trust any web-slinging vigilante. Packed into this moment, then, is an interpretive exit strategy – one where Miles' experience need *not* be deemed unique to his racial identity. And yet, reading the sequence also becomes more difficult without at least some reference to the visual distinctions between the two characters pictured.

Figure 3.4 Miles thrusts Peter B.'s semi-conscious torso against the wall

One is costumed, the other not, their skin color rendered more palpable in the juxtaposition of their open palm submission to the off-screen officers. Miles' dime store Spider-Man suit pops in the light, draped against the muted green of Peter B.'s hipster army fatigue jacket – itself perhaps an indication of his privilege to wear military gear with no fear of arousing suspicion.

In one frame we see both a potential nod to *Weekend at Bernie's* (Ted Kotcheff, 1989) and a well-nigh Althusserian moment of interpolation rendered in inequitable horror, as the abjection of the Black subject emerges in stark contrast to his white counterpart, literally propped up by his efforts, but also his best chance at survival. Put more simply, even though Miles is in his 'own' universe and far less physically imposing than his white counterpart, he is also somehow already less at home – assumed to be more culpable – than Peter B., who has only just arrived. Miles cannot and does not expect the same advantages as his white counterpart – even when he is thrust to the center of his own story. This, the film shows without saying out loud, is a weight much heavier than any inter-dimensional obstacles laid out by the Kingpin and his minions.

What ensues is a madcap chase between the authorities and the conjoined forms of Miles and Peter B., who bounce off walls and cars, eventually latching onto a subway train as it flies through snowy Brooklyn. All throughout, the slapstick nature of the sequence tends to downplay its loaded representational work, much as it did in the prior moments. And yet, as the rhythm of the images offered goes from burst to pause, the physical disparity between the two human bodies also becomes visceral, with the smaller brown Spider-Man alternately lugging and clinging to his lifeless white predecessor, by turns codependent and burdened with his bodyweight. In perhaps the most humorous punchline of the sequence, we cut to a split-second interior shot from a police cruiser just as two officers listen to a message coming over their CB radio, as if to say the quiet part out loud – 'Looks like Spider-Man dragging a homeless corpse behind him'. Meanwhile, Peter B. slowly comes to consciousness, even as his face is repeatedly smashed and dragged into the pavement, as if to render him unrecognizable – or perhaps into a visage resembling characters from *Cloudy with a Chance of Meatballs* (not coincidentally, the previous best-known animated Sony hit by co-producers Lord and Miller).

Finally, as if to completely collapse these possible referents into a composite image, Peter's head is smashed into the uppermost portion of a snowman along the way. Obliquely recalling another shape-shifting sidekick, Olaf the snowman, from *Frozen* (Chris Buck and Jennifer

Lee, 2013), these disparate references are then flattened on the side of a speeding train, viewed momentarily from the inside of the elevated car just as a young Black kid in headphones listens to Belly's 'Mumble Rap' in one of its few family-friendly lyrical moments ('I been riding through this city on my own / Only time I see myself is in this chrome') (see Figure 3.5).

Again, buried in the fray of physical humor and intertexts, we see a series of possible racialized meanings. For 'unknowing' (or disinterested 'knowing') audiences, the physical stunts and change of pace here might be enough already. Indeed, an audible lag in the chorus of the Belly song serves to accentuate the progression of the smashed snow face on the other side of the glass. At the same time, the sequence gives us literal pause to observe an anonymous onlooker, listening to hip hop, alone on public transportation, unaware that someone quite like him meets his eyes from the other side, clinging to the back of the white hero he (and the audience) must follow. Likewise, Belly's words could be 'just' musical filler or comedic content in the scene – a sonic equivalent of the Chance the Rapper poster we see earlier on in Miles' dorm room. Probed for more meaning though, the sequence, like so many others in *The Spider-Verse*, offers much more. Deploying an ironic hierarchy of point-of-view knowledge, the frame encapsulates Miles' struggle for recognition amidst a cacophony of a popular cultural references. His experiences of exclusion remain invisible amidst a flux of generic tropes, despite being laid out in plain sight for those who want to see them. The sequence ends with a long, overhead shot of Miles and Peter B., lying in the snow after dropping from the train to the ground below, with another subtle cameo for Stan Lee (recognizable as one of the many passersby on a second viewing). 'Thank you, Brooklyn', says Miles, with a resigned tone.

Figure 3.5 Disparate references are flattened on the side of a speeding train

The most powerful and affective element in this game of representation, of course, occurs in Miles' primary conflict, dramatized as a choice between masculine role models – Jefferson and Aaron. Whereas the adult male white characters in the film serve as either outright villains (the Kingpin) or comedic sidekicks (Peter B.), the two Black adult male leads are cast with more moral complexity. In the sequences analyzed above, Miles is shown as alternately not fitting in or standing out from his surroundings, with representational cues suggesting racialized content without forcing a choice of interpretive levels. Left as such, the film might be accused of presenting the apparent stakes of racialized representation without making the audience ever *choose* to see race. But even if the audience cannot recognize their vocal qualities from other award-winning roles in *Atlanta* (FX, 2016–22) (Brian Tyree Henry's role as Paper Boi), *Moonlight* and *Green Book* (Peter Farrelly, 2018) (Mahershala Ali's back-to-back Oscars for Supporting Actor), the two characters are given numerous qualities to suggest an opposition between two forms of Black masculinity.

In the comics version of his story, the two brothers were there as well, but Bendis and Pichelli define them less as opposites than as conjoined victims of racial oppression and resistance. In the original *Ultimate Spider-Man* run, they have a criminal backstory, one that Jefferson confesses to Miles in his attempts to wrest him away from Aaron's influence. Yet in that iteration, Jefferson is not a cop, and Aaron's Prowler is revealed earlier on, already hot on Miles' tail after he discovers his nephew has found a radioactive spider he intended to use to develop his own powers. Moreover, the climactic fight between Miles and Aaron concludes with the latter's accidental death, as he burns up due to a malfunction of his own weapons. In Reynolds' novelization of the story, the primary antagonist role is displaced onto the apocalyptic cult run by Miles' History teacher and the white supremacist organization run by the administration.

As described in Chapter 2, Aaron and Jefferson are depicted in starkly different visual and narrative terms in the first act of *The Spider-Verse*. Jefferson is first seen in the bright morning light, scurrying in the background of the Morales apartment, readying for work. As Miles walks to Visions, he code switches with friends, alternating between English and Spanish, slapping his signature tags on various surfaces. For a moment, we see his unlaced Air Jordans, which impede his progress at an inopportune moment, sending him tumbling into the street, right in front of a police cruiser (see Figure 3.6).

Figure 3.6 Miles sprawls in front of a police cruiser

Note that crucial visual information is momentarily impeded by the shot length, as it is again in the subsequent frame, where Miles dejectedly reclines in the back seat, frustrated in the hold of a cop car, allowing for the audience's potential misapprehension to extend. Seconds later, a wider view including the car's driver changes the dynamic, allowing viewers to understand that it is Jefferson, and that Miles' recalcitrance is that of a teenage son to a father, rather than a Black boy to an officer. Moments later, Jefferson pulls up at Visions, using his police car's red-and-blue lights to embarrass Miles in front of his new classmates; 'I love you', he intones. In this public gesture, the declaration of love also serves as an assertion of a Black cop, father to a Black boy about to attend an elite school where he will be a minority.[6]

Aaron, on the other hand, shows up later as an apparent creature of the night, first appearing in the context of his nephew's flight from institutional responsibility, and later as a role model of resistant expression that Miles embraces in defiance of his rule-governed father. Whereas Jefferson struggles to relate to his son – awkwardly pointing out a coffee house as a question of 'kids these days' – his brother seems more at home in the parlance of the times, even teaching his nephew some of his flirting techniques with the eye-contact-shoulder-pat combination he suggests for talking to Wanda/Gwen ('Eh ...'). In the end, this technique will of course return with dramatic irony, becoming the key to Miles' unlocking his Spider Shock power to finally defeat the Kingpin and return Brooklyn to normalcy.

The film is also clever in how it weaves together the racial and super-identities of Aaron and Miles. For the first two-thirds of the film, neither Miles nor Aaron knows that the other is superhuman. Though the Prowler does appear in the first action sequence, responsible for the death of the universe's primary Peter Parker, it is only when Miles goes back to Aaron's apartment in a later scene that he learns of his uncle's hidden identity as the

Kingpin's henchman. Terrified, the boy manages to hide from the menacing purple villain thanks to discovering another power – invisibility. Aaron, for his part, remains ignorant of the new Spider-Man's connection to his nephew until it is too late. Chasing Spider-Man, he finally catches him on a rooftop, lifting him by the neck and removing the mask only to see his nephew's trembling face. When he hesitates, letting Miles go, the flat clap of Kingpin's revolver resounds again. Aaron collapses into an alleyway and the audience is offered, once again, an image with a constellation of possible interpretations. In arguably the film's most tragic sequence though, the collision between racial representation of the two brothers reaches an apex.

The scene is more remarkable if we temporarily wrest it from its immediate narrative context. Cut to an image in an alleyway. In the fore-ground, a gaunt, teenage boy, crouching next to the body of a fallen man. From a high angle perspective, both figures have visibly dark skin, appear to be clad in costumes. The prostrate man wears purple, with a cape; the teen is clad in what appears to be a Spider-Man costume. Clasping his temples in despair, he rumples the mask. Split seconds later, a telltale throb of red-and-blue light seeps into the color palette as a police car passes by, siren sound-ing, framed by the stark verticality of the alley walls (see Figure 3.7).

A few moments pass. Cut to a brief low-angle view of the boy, should-ers heaving, followed by a longer, reverse perspective that hovers over the police officer's shoulder as he exits the car, its mobile frame revealing his larger, uniformed body – also dark skinned – moving with trained preci-sion, unholstering his weapon, straining to glimpse the details we already know about the scene in the alley: 'Hands up! Put your hands up! Now!'

As if to rhyme ironically with the earlier, more playful invocations of police authority, as well as with the train chase sequence discussed earlier,

Figure 3.7 Tragedy in the alleyway

this scene paints tragedy where the previous ones did humor. Miles might potentially be exonerated due to his father's career choice, but here the teen's secret identity – an emerging superhero – makes it impossible for the two to relate at all. Cut briefly back to Miles. He winces, freezes, gradually complies with the police order, then suddenly disappears. The officer, Jefferson, remains alone above the prostrate body, a look of sudden recognition crossing his face. Given what we know in the narrative of *The Spider-Verse*, this prolonged tragedy of mutual misidentification and role reversal is now complete – the dead man is the cop's brother, the boy his son. Jefferson, in these circumstances, is useless to protect either of them. The Prowler's last words – quoted by DuVernay in her tweet – are chillingly emblematic: 'You're the best of us, Miles. You're on your way. Just keep going'.

Even viewed as a brief, five-minute vignette, the scene of Aaron's death would already be loaded with images of Black masculinity that have become tragically too familiar in the history of America, let alone the recent swirl of media misrepresentation. In a culture submerged in the spectacle of crime, punishment, and the threat of police brutality, *The Spider-Verse* could be critiqued for the ways that it poses apparent visual questions without providing answers to them. Yet the film also avoids any easy presentation of moral redemption or salvation. Rather, moments like the one described above let the haunting images of these three characters – Aaron, Jefferson, and Miles – collide, as if to be reckoned with in their full ambivalence without any straightforward conclusions about what to take away.

'You Gotta Choose a Side'

As if to further emphasize the layer of racialized meaning that this chapter has been advocating for, the closing credits of the film offer an effective music video for DJ Khaled's 'Elevate', accompanied by visuals that dramatize, in slightly different form, the active mode of viewership that the film has just demonstrated throughout its runtime. Just one of numerous catchy tracks from the film's original soundtrack, the song takes over right after Miles settles into his bed, hands clasped behind his head, with pastel-colored Kirby Krackle visuals floating above. The audience has just witnessed, at long last, Miles' own version of the 'My name is …' montage, which rewards them by rehashing their own knowledge of the film, but this time making Miles' story the point of reference rather than a glut of fictionalized paratexts referenced by the first Peter Parker at the outset of the film (see Chapter 1) or his white doppelganger, Peter B. Instead, a summary of characters and events that the audience has just watched themselves both affirms Miles as the hero of his *own* story – 'Anyone can wear the mask' – and rewards viewers for persevering through two hours of references they may or may not know. Anyone, it would seem to say, can also *understand* a film as complex as *The Spider-Verse*.

The credit sequence offers another, more abstract iteration of these same themes of interpretation and representation. In a sort of flowing, geometric onslaught of an entirely different kind, it presents a collage of serialized, animated Spider-Men dances, with numerous costumed figures contorting, leaping, and gyrating in and out of a two-dimensional landscape, timed to the infectious beats of 'Elevate' by Khaled and his four collaborators, Denzel Curry, YBN Cordae, SwaVay, and T. Rich. Credits are superimposed over these sequences, sometimes in the form of slap tags resembling the ones Miles creates earlier in the film or in the form of comic-style captions (see Chapter 2). Likely an oblique nod to Michelle Obama's famous assertion during her husband's 2012 Presidential campaign about how to counter personal attacks from political opponents ('They go low, we go high'), the chorus repeats each phrase twice, as if to evoke echoes or, more proximately, the narrator's internalized form of affirmative call and response: 'They wanna fight? / I'm just gonna let 'em hate / Gotta go high / I gotta elevate'.

The lyrics are suitably ambivalent – offering no prescriptive target for what 'hate' or obstacles the speaker faces, hence leaving room for a universalized interpretation. And as the viewer watches various Spider-Men flying by in varying styles and on different visual planes, weaving in lines and other formations, in and out of the depths of rolling Ben-Day littered surfaces, different incarnations of Spider-bodied figures emerge, each recalling the different textures of the multiverse as presented in the film that came before. All the major characters appear at some point, usually accompanied by graphics that resemble the ones they were shown with before or recalling their role in the narrative proper – often both.

Various scenes from Miles' adventure also appear in a kind of miniaturized format – the 'No Expectations' graffiti spray art he created with his uncle surfaces as a kind of frieze; the 'Hey!' moment where he transmits his 'Spider shock' power cascades in a triangular set of split-screen shapes behind a blown-up Spider-Man figure extending his arm. As they by turns resemble Busby Berkeley dance choreography, or the famous 'mirror' image of Charlie at the conclusion of *Citizen Kane*, or an animated Lilliputian landscape redolent of Swiftian satire, the kaleidoscope of scenes also thematize certain disparities amidst the red-and-blue clad figures, which flood everywhere, by the end becoming part of a latticed pattern that takes over the images. In their midst, by far the minority, black-clad figures are included here and there, in some places facing comedic forms of physical exclusion that seem to single them out – a gargantuan Spider-Ham 'whack-a-mole' hammer slams one of them into the ground.

At another moment, a series of nametags resembling the ones Miles used in his neighborhood appears on screen. A black-suited figure leaps across them, showing Miles' trajectory across 'My name is …' name-tag surfaces, but making his bodily trajectory resemble a haphazard ink stain. This is followed by an apparent panel border, which in the context of a moving image also resembles a horizontal wipe, and a fist that seems to be raising its hand in some sort of protest. Lest anyone think that gesture might invoke something related to social or even racial protest — recalling perhaps John Carlos and Tommy Smith at the 1968 Olympics – a second gesture immediately appears to the right, index and pinky fingers raised instead. As if to diffuse the first thought (protest) with another meaning entirely ('rock on'), the image track moves to an apparent concert scene led by Gwen Stacy and her band. Meanwhile, in the background, lower screen right, the opaque white eyeholes of single black-clad figure peer out at the audience, nearly hidden in a sea of red-and-blue costumes and limbs (see Figure 3.8).

On one level, none of this is unexpected. Marvel's other live action superhero films have for years conditioned audiences to read closing sequences intertextually, not to mention the visual variations offered during many recent Pixar and DreamWorks credits. Moreover, all the figures involved are wearing Spider-suits and there are far more references included in the sequence than the ones that seem to single out the black-clad figures. In other words, the particularized reading of

Figure 3.8 Multiple connotations unfurl in the closing credit sequence

racial symbolism remains marginal here, as if constantly under threat with less polemical options. Ramsey and his colleagues are clearly not in the business of making overtly political cinema, instead often burying the logic of a racialized critique in the barrage of visual and sonic elements that comprise their inventive animated feature.

Yet the racialized discourse of the film, or the nascent possibility for it, remains even still – in this case thematized as a choice. Just as the featured secondary rappers on the DJ Khaled song launch into their even faster, syncopated rhyme schemes, the imagery of the closing credits could suggest visually that the 'sides' to which the song refers involve different ways to interpret the flux of representations on the screen; in other words, this is a choice to read for difference. However, as if to answer potential interpretive quandaries, a second catchline directly follows up the first one in the song, a sort of call-and-response rejoinder, not necessarily compatible with earlier calls to 'elevate' above the fray, and without any ethical ambiguity: 'You gotta do what's right'.

Conclusion

The Spider-Verse leaves the viewer with a strong residual impression of its main teenage character, of the challenges he faces, and of what recognizing his struggle with respect to contemporary media forms might entail. Immersed in this multidimensional game of plausibly deniable pop culture signifiers, the film could be critiqued for marginalizing its Afro-Latino hero amidst other characters (Jeffries 2022). Yet as this analysis has shown, this is also a film that nevertheless keeps beckoning its audiences to *read* racially – even when the evidence seems hidden in plain sight.

As Miles grows in confidence, he further embraces his own role as a universe-hopper, ready to flout naysayers or systemic obstacles with knowing charisma and interpretive flexibility. In this way, the film ends its runtime not with Obama's high-minded avoidance tactics ('we go high') or Xendi's anti-racist thought experiments, but with a sequence that complements these frames with another tack, more fitting for its youthful protagonist – flexible, adaptable, multifaceted – with the sort of postmodern sensibility proposed by theorists like Cornel West, who critique the binary limits of the 'double consciousness' characterized so many years ago by W.E.B. Du Bois.[7] Moreover, when the self-actualized lyrics of *The Spider-Verse* soundtrack rhyme schematically with its cascade of imagery, the film also conjures something like a contemporary youth sensibility, where a flippant response of cavalier courage – 'What's Up Danger?' – seems primed to face down whatever mutable forms the specter of racial oppression might take next.

Notes

1 I am grateful to Ayanni Hanna for her insights on Miles' fashion sense and its relationship to Black boyhood, which were presented in an unpublished SCMS paper on the panel 'Untangling the Spider-Verse' in March 2022.

2 Spike Lee's Brooklyn – depicted in so many of his memorable and masterful joints – could be cited as a general intertext for numerous aspects of this film as well.

3 *The 1619 Project* is Nikole Hannah-Jones' ongoing, long-form, journalistic account of US history with respect to slavery. Winner of the Pulitzer Prize in 2020, it is perhaps the best known of the numerous contributions to a growing progressive-minded literature on the contemporary legacy of slavery and how it affects race relations in the US. These include titles like *Uncomfortable Conversations with a Black Man* (Emmanuel Ache, 2021), *Mediocre: The Dangerous Legacy of White Male America* (Ijeama Oluo, 2021), *The Sum of Us: What Racism Costs Everyone and How We Can Prosper Together* (Heather McGhee, 2021) and many other titles.

4 Much to the consternation of political elites, Trump's legions of red-and-white hatted followers continue their rampage to this day, in a call for a return to a pre-Civil Rights America of the 1950s that has made him the leading Republican candidate for 2024 despite multiple criminal indictments.

5 I draw some of this analysis for how the Kingpin fosters a foil of whiteness for the other white characters from Russell Meeuf, who pointed them out in an unpublished SCMS paper in a panel called 'Untangling the Spider-Verse' in March 2021.

6 As James Baldwin reminds us, Black cops in the US have historically dealt with an impossible position – trying to prove themselves to their white counterparts while serving their own community (Baldwin 1985: 50).

7 For an in-depth reading of how this emergent sensibility plays out in terms of Spike Lee's *Do the Right Thing* (1989) see McKelly (2007).

Conclusion
'Which one pointed first?'

The last image of *Spider-Man: Into the Spider-Verse* – like so many others in the film – arguably does not come from *this* movie at all. In a post-credit scene, yet *another* Spider-Man appears. Details here are initially somewhat difficult to parse, but the audience eventually gleans that this new character is called Miguel (voiced by Oscar Isaac), and that he and Lyla, his petite hologram assistant, are preparing an 'autonomous multiverse jump' to take him to yet *another* dimension. She asks where he would like to go, and he says 'Back to the very beginning. Let's do this one last time – Earth-67'.

Once they get there, the visual field is presented in a different style with a smaller aspect ratio and a graphic quality that resembles cell animation – flatter with more muted colors and thicker lines than any we have seen prior. Even if all audience members cannot identify the design of the original animated *Spider-Man* television show (ABC, 1967–70), they will at least note its visual distinctions from the CGI contours of the previous images – and the more general evocation of going 'still elsewhere' in the Spider-Verse. Inevitably, moments later Miguel runs into another red-and-blue clad hero – the Spider-Man from *that* world. 'I'm Spider-Man and I am from the future', proclaims Miguel. At that point, the two characters pause for a beat, confused, looking at each other, and then start pointing – eventually accusing each other of being rude for the gesture (see Figure 4.1). Cut to a bemused police officer looking on this absurdist exercise with an honest question – 'Which one pointed first?' – at which point the animated 1967 version of *Daily Bugle* magnate J. Jonah Jameson appears, bellowing in his eternally-cranky way that it was 'Spider-Man, obviously!' The film ends, then, not by concluding the arc of Miles Morales, but with a fragmentary episode that literally gestures, again, to the *elsewhere* – to other characters, another world.

DOI: 10.4324/9781003166962-5

Figure 4.1 Miguel O'Hara meets his alter-ego from the past

As with so many other moments of *The Spider-Verse,* interpretive mileage may vary with this scene. Devoted fans will recognize Miguel O'Hara, who first appeared as an alternative hero called 'Spider-Man 2099' in 1992 as part of the *Marvel 2099* imprint – a series which imagined futuristic versions of its most popular heroes. Others might recognize the 'old school' design of Miguel's dimensional destination, which mimics the look of the original animated *Spider-Man* television show, which ran for 53 episodes on ABC in the late 1960s, endowing the franchise with its most memorable theme song in the process (Raymond 2023). Upon inspection, the details of Figure 4.1 are almost identical to the original television frame, which presents two figures in front of a pale, pink wall with a white-lettered NYPD paddy wagon, screen-left, and a non-descript pile of boxes, screen-right. A conspicuous difference in *The Spider-Verse* version, of course, is that Miguel is now the figure on the left – a darker navy suit and a distinctive red patterning on his mask.

There are some practical reasons for why Miguel O'Hara is excluded from the main story of the first *Spider-Verse* film. Like Miles, he is a multiracial character – an Irish-Mexican lab engineer who works at Alchemax on Earth-928, which is presented in the comics storyline as a possible future version of Earth-616, Spider-Man's original home. In 1992, he thus became the first non-exclusively white hero to don the mask, some two decades before Bendis and Pichelli created Miles. But unlike Peter, Miles, and their other friends from the movie, the development of Miguel's powers is not the result of a happenstance spider bite. Rather, they derive from misbegotten experiments at Alchemax.

When a test subject is killed in genetic-splicing trials with animal DNA, Miguel tries to expose the lab's corrupt methods, only to have his supervisor sabotage him by injecting his body with an addictive serum called 'Rapture'. Desperate to escape Alchemax's control, Miguel instead turns the genetic splicing process on himself, curing his 'Rapture' addiction but suffering multiple mutations as a result. Later, while his emerging web-slinging skills and athletic prowess suggest he might be a new 'Spider-Man', he also endures physical changes like fangs and talons, and mental powers like telepathy and night vision that were never associated with Peter Parker. At one point, Miguel even jokes that his he is so different from his predecessors that he might as well be called 'Santa Claus' or the 'Easter Bunny' instead.

Much like the cascade of references in Peter Parker's opening voice-over montage, the final scene makes a layered gesture at other memorable moments in the Spider-Man canon. The 'pointing' episode repeats a pattern common to the rest of the film – a Spider-Hero travels inter-dimensionally, encounters another version of 'himself' and, as before, the meanings derived from that interaction depend on the audience's familiarity with the character's fictional variations and afterlives. Seasoned viewers will recognize the roots of a tradition where cliff-hanger endings and alternate plotlines have long been a staple – whether in the pulpy sound serials from matinee movie screenings (Higgins 2016) or in the superhero tradition that Marvel helped create (Brinker 2022). For their part, Stan Lee and Steve Ditko made a memorable move toward serialized plotting in Spider-Man a few years after the character's introduction. In a three-issue plotline from *The Amazing Spider-Man* (1965–1966), Spider-Man finds himself in dire straits at the end of issue #32. Submerged in encroaching water and trapped under heavy machinery with his leg badly injured, Peter summons a last-gasp effort to escape and – in an iconic spread of panels from issue #33 – pulls himself from the wreckage by imagining the peril of his Aunt May, who has just been captured. As with the death of Uncle Ben and the 'great responsibility' tropes from his debut, the desperate events from the 'If this be my destiny ...' plot (a phrase featured on the cover of #31) have been recounted numerous times since their first appearance, including serving as the basis for *The Amazing Spider-Man 2* and, with slight variations, for the climax of *Spider-Man: Homecoming*.

While none of these details are essential for a general understanding of his final scene, Miguel's closing cameo also stands apart from the rest of *The Spider-Verse* in other important ways. Notably, in this case the film does not provide the requisite safeguards for basic comprehension. Gone are Peter Parker's encouraging words ('Let's do this one last time...') and his self-deprecating ridicule of Christmas albums and melting popsicles from the opening voiceover sequences. Absent too are the more obvious common denominators like the upside-down kiss from *Spider-Man*, for instance (see Chapter 1). No one reassures the audience that they should (or even could) 'know the rest'; there is no safety net for 'unknowing' audiences (Hutcheon 2012). Instead, it is as if the sequence is put here to defy the very possibility of mastering all reference points – or even a sort of absurdist punchline about all of the above. This interpretive tack is thematized by the empty gestures of two characters, who seem to be engaged in a perpetual game of deferred self-recognition – pointing. On this view, the closing impression becomes one of inexhaustible meanings – and feckless, never-ending repetition.

Continually pointing at an elsewhere – but also at itself – the final confrontation between Miguel and this anonymous 'other' Spider-Man gestures at larger meanings, beyond Miles Morales. Thrusting the viewer into an amorphous, electronically contrived place between worlds, *The Spider-Verse* evokes the online world through its glitch-ridden surface textures, its polyphony of animated worlds, and its pluralistic cast of characters. Hierarchy itself seems threatened under these circumstances. For whatever an audience's knowledge of previous Spider-lore, many will experience the film not as an historical parade of 'primary' to 'secondary' Spider-People, but rather as a constant accumulation of the possible, where there is no definable 'first' image at all. Characters, worlds, and plot variations swirl around in the ether, often without clear attribution, and usually difficult to track to their origins. A term like 'hypertext' may therefore seem rather callow here, given contemporary forms of cultural exchange that seem to traipse across endless virtual paths – from YouTube to TikTok, Instagram to X (formerly Twitter), and Reddit to Facebook – rehashing and reappropriating the meaning of the image *ad infinitum*. In this light, Miguel O'Hara's cameo in the first *Spider-Verse* rings not as any finality, but as a suggestion that the film's borders are as indiscriminately porous and changeable as ever.

Continuations

It is difficult to propose any definitive conclusions about a movie as expansive and propulsive as *The Spider-Verse*. As the final episode with Miguel seems to suggest, few audience members can even hope to track the constant ricochet of references. By the time these words are published, at least one sequel to the film will be available on streaming queues, with another one on the way to finish a trilogy that will populate screens large and small with even more versions of Miles – not to mention the innumerable pages, panels, toy shelves, and theme parks that will redouble his adventures in forms large and small. From this perspective, the inexhaustible, mirrored dynamics of digital networks themselves seem to be the expressive frontier for this film, which evokes the overwhelming size and scope of contemporary image culture through the experiences of a self-effacing teen protagonist. No doubt, the ongoing life of Miles and his friends from *The Spider-Verse* sequels will soon themselves have progressed well beyond the confines of the original details described here, borne on a flood of licensed productions, spinoffs, and product tie-ins from Sony, Marvel, and their partners, but also on the proliferation of unlicensed and fan-created media, which has flourished online since the popularity of the first film, reinforcing *The Spider-Verse* as a continual point of reference for both animation style and the superhero genre.

As described in previous chapters, one of the notable features of *The Spider-Verse* is that it is made to be readable within and among variable levels of knowledge and angles of interpretation. Take Miguel's cameo, for instance. Positioned at the end of the credits, the final episode of the film arrives just before (or in some cases during) the waning of attention spans – a reality of how meaning is generated in the age of social media. Moreover, for many younger viewers of *The Spider-Verse*, closing with this decentralized encounter with the 'pointing' episode will have little to do with the film they have just watched, with Spider-Man 2099, or with the 1960s television show. Rather, it will kindle their familiarity with a viral internet meme that first spread in the 2010s, before Lord, Miller, and their colleagues had even heard of Miles Morales. In those days, the same image from a 'doppelganger' episode of the 1960s *Spider-Man* television show had already made rounds on internet feeds, known colloquially as the 'Spider-Man Pointing at Spider-Man' meme (Adam 2018). The image resurfaced repeatedly on social media, most often appended to posts as a humorous shorthand for the irony of misrecognition. First a screen grab from the television original, the still image of two pointing Spider-Man figures, as with all meme culture, became transportable and mutable, moving to numerous other contexts – from political discussion threads (say to evoke the hypocrisy of public adversaries guilty of similar transgressions) to sports fandom forums (ideal for observing the resemblance between two players or teams generally assumed to be different).

Since the release of *The Spider-Verse* and its subsequent success, the 'pointing' meme has circled all the way back once more, resurfacing as marketing tactic for the late 2010s franchise entries, but now a hip strategy for appealing to Spider-Man's own redundancy as a character. Given the longstanding collaboration between Disney's Feige and Sony's Pascal and Arad, it can be no accident that the episode gained more currency with the appearance of a third instalment in Marvel's concurrent live-action franchise. Embracing the multiverse conceit much like its animated precursor, *Spider-Man: No Way Home* (2021) mobilizes all three stars of the live action *Spider-Man* franchises of the 2000s (Tobey Maguire, Andrew Garfield, Tom Holland), repurposing the 'pointing' meme in February 2023 as part of the marketing campaign.[1] In the plot of *No Way Home*, Holland's Parker inadvertently disrupts the time-space continuum, bringing two other Parkers (Garfield and Maguire) to his world, along with the villains from their respective films. In the end, the Spider-Man of *No Way Home* must risk his human relationships with MJ and Ned to 'reboot' his world and send the time-tripping villains back to their dimensions before they destroy his own. The end of *No Way Home* certainly anticipates the consequences of irresponsible multiplicity, leaving Peter with the unenviable task of rebuilding his human relationships – even reconstructing his origin story – in future films. At the same time, his task presupposes the possible rebuilding of a 'center', while the ending of *The Spider-Verse* leaves us with a more anarchic, unstable conclusion.

At the time of writing, the two *Spider-Verse* sequels sit poised to maximize the thematic and financial potential of this type of commentary. Miguel's moment at the end of the first film is the first inkling the audience gets of what is to come. *Spider-Man: Across the Spider-Verse*, released to theatres in June 2023, garnered rapturous critical and box office returns. As if to honor the spirit of collaboration already present throughout the first film, Ramsey and his colleagues ceded the sequel's directorial credit to another trio of animators who participated in the first film – Justin K. Thompson, Joaquim Dos Santos, and Kemp Powers. Teaser trailers for the second film doubled down on the pointing meme, offering revealing glimpses of what looks like a labyrinthine world, populated by innumerable red-and-blue clad figures pointing at one another, suggesting a mass reproduction of representatives from various 'subcreated' worlds (Wolf 2012).

An extended consideration of the plot and features of the two sequels would be outside the scope of this book. The author also writes the previous sentence while duly noting its irony – given how self-aware the film itself is in about the dynamics of its own fictional excesses.

That said, it bears observing that the second film does embrace an even more extreme style, where meme-ified worldbuilding and reflexive storytelling rollick on the screen as few films do. Here is a franchise that is aware of how meaning is created and deployed in a culture that left older, text-based forms behind some time ago. The other irony, of course, is that texts always 'point' elsewhere, whatever their medium of choice. Where does that leave a film which, in its most dynamic moments, anticipates and expresses the experiences of a youth audience also poised to leap into this sort of technological beyond?

Ineffable and often non-narrative, memes could be an example of a recent textual phenomenon that either amplifies Genette's concept of hypertext – or obliterates it. If the titles of the films in the *Spider-Verse* franchise sound academic, brandishing their use of colons in a conceptual way that few blockbusters do, that is because they share in a language that stretches to accommodate energies that evade customary containment of time and space, putting strain on the parts of speech that express the defined dimensionality and centripetal movement of texts in the more contained, classical sense of narrative form. This accounts for the prepositions that differentiate the titles of the films in the trilogy, which seem to propose trajectories for the hero (but also the viewer) that move, respectively, *into, across,* and eventually *beyond* the worlds depicted on-screen. In other words, the experience of this movie is, ultimately, not about *this* or *that* movie at all.

To align *The Spider-Verse* with the experiences of young people, then, also means acknowledging the ways in which the aesthetic features of the film try to express the energy and abandon of how contemporary youth culture itself functions. For this viewer, one of the pleasures of going 'into' *The Spider-Verse* is that the film both internally and externally expresses an experience of navigating the present media environment. These dynamics also constitute one of the challenges of writing about a film like this one. It is as if the very act of describing Miles Morales demands a constant grappling with an online *Spider-Verse* 'hive mind', evergreen with new content uploaded almost every day, be it video essays, blog posts, playlists, or play-through videos. Produced at all levels of institutional verifiability and fan expertise, these resources offer an invaluable research tool (see the numerous notes and citations from this book) even while their sheer number also threatens to overwhelm at every turn.

Some of these additions to the Miles-Verse are commercialized, and that begins with the feature film sequels and their story arcs. Meanwhile, the franchise continues to thematize its own dynamics of sub-creation at all levels, maximizing the game between 'authorized' and 'unauthorized' property, and relating it to the cultural politics of racial identity more broadly. Released as this book was being finalized, *Across the Spider-Verse* brought these dynamics starkly to life once more, maximizing the tie-in opportunities that had been largely absent for its lower profile predecessor. In a flourish befitting the thematic and creative tendencies of the first film, *Across the Spider-Verse* turns on a narrative about the tyranny of Miguel's interpretive powers and the primacy of his own 'alternative' origin story. The first racially alternative Spider-Man, it turns out, remains so scarred by his own misfortune that he fears the consequences of widespread deviations from the normative 'great responsibility' story arc. That reading of the hero's journey – the one re-rehearsed many times in the first film – mandates *only one* Spider-Person per world, and a story that turns on the untimely death of someone close to him or her (Uncle Ben for Peter Parker, Captain Stacy for his daughter Gwen, etc., etc.). With righteous indignation, the Miguel of *Across the Spider-Verse* rails against all Spider-Folk who otherwise alter their canonical roles, leading an underground 'Spider Society' designed to prevent all variations from straying too far from this pattern. Miles, for Miguel, violates the canonical version because he comes from a world where Peter already existed; he is therefore an 'anomaly' that must be eliminated – in this case held hostage – to prevent further dire outcomes.

In 2023, awaiting a third film in the aftermath of the second one's successful box office, *The Spider-Verse* has clearly ascended to the status of a full-fledged multimedia franchise. Of course, the first film already boasted a plethora of tie-ins, which escalated after its 2018 release – action figures, Lego sets, spinoff comic imprints, children's and adult's clothing, a PlayStation video game. But the second film's launch was timed in a more saturated way, further in concert with the sorts of products that Peter Parker actually mocks in the introductory 'My name is …' passage of the first film, where this book began. New tie-ins range in quality from a thoughtful follow-up youth novel by Jason Reynolds called *Suspended* (released in May 2023) to – perhaps most garish of all – a new signature menu item at Burger King called the 'Spider-Verse Whopper', presented to hungry customers complete with a dyed-red bun (Guzman 2023).

Meanwhile, Miles and other 'diverse' heroes have become a hinge point for Marvel's ongoing outreach to different audiences in their comics. A recent spinoff issue from Marvel Comics, *How to Read Comics the Marvel Way* (Hastings 2022) makes Spider-Man the face of a campaign to teach new readers the formal elements of comic books. Much like Scott McCloud's work (1994), the premise of this Marvel

'How To' primer revolves around using the formal elements of paneled storytelling to both teach readers the basics of narrative comprehension and acquaint them with their character options. To this end, Spider-Man graces the cover, swinging through dialogue bubbles ('I'll get you Spider-Man ...') and narrative captions ('Meanwhile ...') as if the physical mobility of the web-slinging character embodies the formal features of paneled storytelling itself. The ensuing tutorial features Spider-Man in his suit, but never unmasks him to reveal a racial or ethnic identity. Although Peter Parker does eventually star in the first story chronologically – presented midway through the collection after the tutorial – his adventure is closely followed by Miles, who appears in a reprint of his origin story in *Ultimate Fallout* #4, followed by Kamala Khan, the teenage, Pakistani protégé of Captain Marvel. Both Miles and Kamala also feature as ongoing members of a rebooted series of Marvel comics called 'New Champions', where younger, more ethnically diverse, teen protagonists form a team based on a collective distancing from the heroes of previous generations.[2]

Of course, not all the various uses for *The Spider-Verse* have been of the authorized or commercialized variety. Like so much of contemporary popular culture, the film's ongoing evocations usually fall somewhere in the creative uncertainty between convulsive studio cash grabs and the endless fan-made iterations of its enduring 'greatness' online. In the years since its release, sequences from the film surface continually in the ephemera of internet image culture, in what has become a voluminous reservoir of information – encyclopedic appreciations of Miles and the film on Wikipedia and Fandom.com; blog posts both personal and corporate-driven; 'Best Of' rankings from all sorts of sources; video essays from college students and professional content creators; animation 'How To' guides in both print and video form. These combined resources, alternatively helping to write this book and threatening its subject matter with redundancy, are part of what it currently means to leap 'into' *The Spider-Verse* – or any other recent specimen of youth culture at-large.

One of the more enduring sub-segments of *Spider-Verse* media online currently relates to another prominent group of paratexts that has been largely beyond the scope of this volume – video games. Arguably the first audio-visual appearances of 'alternative' Spider-Man characters with a multiverse framing, the action-adventure game *Spider-Man: Shattered Dimensions* was first developed by the firm Beenox and released by Activision in 2010. The game featured four playable alternates of Spider-Man in their own dimensions (Amazing, 2099, Ultimate, and Noir), but fell prey to the same licensing upheaval as the feature films did in 2014, when Sony's contract with Activision was discontinued (along with its larger arrangement with Marvel). Two years after *The Spider-Verse* film, a PlayStation game called *Marvel's Spider-Man: Miles Morales* was developed by Insomniac Games, first released for the PS4 and as a launch title for PS5 in November 2020 (Keane 2020).

In some senses, the game has a more conventional canonical hierarchy than the Miles movies, as there is never any question about its subordinate status – it is a direct spinoff of the PlayStation title *Marvel's Spider-Man*, which launched in 2018 for the PS4. On one hand the *Miles Morales* game's clear secondary status to the original deprives it of some of the novelties of his appearance in *The Spider-Verse* film. Gameplay is largely similar to its Parker-centric predecessor, which has the same open-world design and play controls for the character. In the narrative of the game, Miles has just finished training for a year with Peter Parker in Earth-1048 (the world depicted in the previous game). His achievements in the sequel depend on following in his mentor's legacy while acquiring the new powers that are different from Peter – the same shock strike ('Venom') and invisibility ('Camouflage') he masters in other versions of the story (comics, novel, and movie). However, any hierarchy between the two games is also primarily extratextual, as players of *Spider-Man: Miles Morales* can proceed with their game without necessarily knowing about past events. Here, experiencing a story centered almost completely on a new Afro-Latino hero does not involve sustained reckoning with plural dimensions or worlds. Rather, Miles is the central figure, and he is accompanied by a plot and a cast of characters meant to support him – including his Korean chum, Ganke, who assists Miles with tech as he did in the *Miles Morales* novel and comics, and Phin Mason, another childhood friend who, much like Uncle Aaron, is revealed to have a secret, villainous alter-ego.

Since the release of *Marvel's Spider-Man: Miles Morales*, the copresence of the game's narrative alongside the series of *Spider-Verse* feature films serves as a case in point for relevance of the last 'pointing' episode. On an initial search of YouTube thumbnails, for instance, it is often difficult to tell the difference between the graphics of the game and the animation of the movie – at least at first glance. Audiences will invariably encounter different screen iterations of Miles and his adventures everywhere, so much so that discerning any 'primary' version of events in his story arc seems to be increasingly beside the point. This is even more true since the release of the second film, which made clear the extent to which the film franchise will also reflexively refer to the power dynamics inherent to any sort of gatekeeping against the spread of 'unauthorized' expansions.

While the *Miles Morales* videogame release came two years after the first *Spider-Verse* film, *Across the Spider-Verse* draws more heavily on the popularity of the games, even thematizing the power relationships between themselves and their 'secondary' texts. Among other Easter Eggs, the Spider Society features a character called 'Insomniac Spider-Man of Earth-1048' as one of Miguel's many encased 'anomaly' characters, as well as a brief tussle between Peter B. and a fighting 'Spider-Cat' who appeared in the first *Marvel's Spider-Man* game. The more significant repercussion of small references like these, however, might be the burgeoning creative work of actual 'unauthorized' creators, many of them gamers who alongside dozens of detailed 'play-through' videos of the *Miles Morales* game, have now uploaded other content. These range from critical analyses of Miles' various suits in the game ('All Miles Main Spider-Verse Suits ...' 2023), to side-by-side comparisons between the different versions of the game ('Spider-Man Remastered ... 2023), to slavish imitation – as seen in one user's use of the video game to recreate the 'What's Up Danger' leap-of-faith scene from the movie frame by frame ('"What's Up Danger" Scene ...' 2022).

In all this, *The Spider-Verse* and its embrace of multiple dimensions seem poised to become a model, not only for the MCU and its ongoing line of feature films, but also for the ways in which other franchises might seek to market products to a rising generation of youthful consumers. Never shy to capitalize on a new trend, Hollywood seems determined to offer every kind of multiverse combination these days, especially since that form of narration promises the expedient creation of more possible extensions. After *The Spider-Verse* and *Spider-Man: No Way Home* came Marvel's *Shang-Chi and the Legend of the Ten Rings* and *Dr. Strange and the Multiverse of Madness* – to name but a few. Meanwhile, outside of the MCU, competitors rush to keep up, dreaming of parallel DC multiverses in *Batman v. Superman: Dawn of Justice* (Zach Snyder, 2016) or *The Flash*, or of launching the *Harry Potter* prequels and sequels. All these titles, to some extent, draw on their own hypertextual 'roller decks' – maximizing previous versions to rework age-old plot points while deploying strategic nods to those entries in a way that appeals to hard-earned fan knowledge of hypotext. Yet none of them slaloms more successfully between hypertextual layers during its very run-time than *The Spider-Verse* – which uses the ensuing intrigue to mount a parallel meditation on the representational dynamics of the very cultural forms it celebrates.

Closing Gestures

In its innovative use of pluralistic animation and citational styles, *Spider-Man: Into the Spider-Verse* condenses – and thereby elaborates on – the extensional forms of narrative used in other recent examples of 'transmedia storytelling'. A cornerstone of the argument presented in these pages has been to understand the energies of this work as *hypertextual* – an adjective used here to refer both to how this movie feels and how it works – convulsively referring to, frequently inverting, and sometimes even inventing its own system of referential meaning (*hypotext*) (Chapter 1). To substantiate this claim analytically, this book looks at two of these layers, first showing how different animation styles comingle to create further reference points (Chapter 2), then considering how those formal elements also serve to emphasize various racialized resonances throughout the film's run time (Chapter 3). A connective tissue between these ideas has been that *The Spider-Verse*'s referential style also balances the needs of different types of viewers, offering sequences that both reward the knowledge of devoted fans and educate less-familiar viewers about the annals of previous Spider-lore. The repeated spider-bite origin stories, for instance, serve both to present basic information and to teach general audiences *how* to read them. This acquired knowledge is then rewarded by the penultimate montage sequence, where Miles repeats it again – becoming, at long last, 'the one and only Spider-Man'. Arrangements like these serve to balance the differential experiences of what Linda Hutcheon calls 'knowing' and 'unknowing' audiences (2012).

At the end of the film, however, the audience is pulled in both directions – as the story gestures towards closure and multiplicity in equal measure. Embedding Easter Eggs – or what Gérard Genette would call *hypotext* – as a reward for some viewers acknowledges past episodes and characters, helping the film celebrate a new Spider-Man in a universally readable style, but also welcoming further analysis and scrutiny by fans. As Miguel's closing vignette also seems to parody though, no audience interpretation of a work can ever quite *contain* the possible pluralities of meaning – or of Spider-People – no matter how aware it (or they) may be of their own 'pointing' gestures. Indeed, what makes *The Spider-Verse* so exciting (and perplexing) at times is that the film both derives *from* and thrives *on* its own multitude of relationships to 'other' works – or as Genette calls them, *paratexts*. Previous chapters of this volume make the case for mapping these elements in different ways, reading between and among them in a manner that outlines how the film comments on its own modes of expression.

As discussed in Chapter 2, recent scholars have developed a language to refer to how contemporary media franchises like this one craft their stories in anticipation of audiences that can and do move freely between and among numerous types of media. And yet, theorists of transmedia also freely acknowledge that the 'secondary' works produced for today's mainstream film franchises do not always bow to the primacy of a main work or 'mothership' (Jenkins 2009; Gray 2010; Mittell 2015; Meikle 2019). *The Spider-Verse* is that rare text that both activates and represents the energy therein without losing its way. There is evidence that a far more chaotic vision of this world existed in pre-production. In interviews, Perischetti and his creative partners describe a first version of the screenplay that embraced the chaotic expansion of multi-dimensionality (O'Connell, 2022: 211–25). That their final version of the film pulled back from these tendencies attests to Sony's commitment to market norms – but also to the filmmakers' concern with telling a coherent story about their main character, whose nervous enthusiasm and self-deprecating charisma remain a rare and authentic screen form of 'Black boy joy' that so many critics rightly celebrate (Eschoe 2018).

Where does this leave the audience? One could do worse than Miles himself. After bidding farewell to his interdimensional cohort, the youthful protagonist closes his eyes, arms folded behind his head as he listens to headphones (the recognizable lilt of Post Malone and Swae Lee's 'Sunflower' returns). The Kingpin defeated, the multiverse saved for now, Miles relaxes, at last able to contemplate his achievements, his ascension to 'wear the mask'. Notably, the audience is not quite as privy to the character's thoughts as they were in so many earlier evocations of his adolescent awkwardness. Perhaps he dreams of a budding romance with Gwen, or other possible futures. In any case, the central sensibility of the film no longer seems perturbed by the Kirby Krackle, which swirls above his head now, apparently more contained to possible subjective realms instead of causing a vexing split in the time-space continuum.

Like the grinning hero they have just met, viewers of *The Spider-Verse* might also rest more easily here. Previously submerged in a cascade of Easter Eggs, they emerge here unscathed, enjoying the conventional pleasure of narrative closure – perhaps even basking in a newfound mastery of the Spider-Man canon. And yet, Miguel's post-credit cameo also threatens this delicate new balance, giving *The Spider-Verse* a clever way to signal the eventual insufficiency of its own premise. As playful as it first might appear, the 'Spider-Man points at Spider-Man' meme strikes at the pressure points of a coming-of-age story where the depiction of authentic cultural experience perches on an inexhaustible tension between 'inside' and 'outside' audience knowledge. Read in this way, the convulsive gestures of a thrice-reappropriated 1960s television cartoon indicate both the serialized roots of the Spider-Man character and its potential futures in the multitude. Anyone hoping to leap successfully into, across – or beyond? – such fulsome iconographic landscapes will also have to thrive on the uncertainty of a citational style where generational and chronological hierarchies have become more difficult than ever to ascertain. If more heroes like Miles Morales are a result of that sea change, everyone may eventually be better off for it.

Notes

1 The earlier spread of the meme has been duly chronicled by the useful online enclave KnowYourMeme.com, which traces its birth to 2011 with a few tweets, picking up steam in the mid-teens, especially with reference to hip hop music and culture (see Adam 2018).

2 During its runtime between 2016 and 2021, the 'New Champions' team included a series of revisionist teenage 'legacy' heroes who either replaced or displaced older figures from the Earth-616 canon of the comics – Kamala Khan (Ms. Marvel), Amadeus Cho (Brawn aka 'New Hulk'), Riri Williams (Iron Man's protégé Ironheart) and Viv Vision (daughter of Vision), among others. At the time of writing, both Kamala Khan (*The Marvels* [Nia DaCosta, 2013]) and Riri Williams (*Wakanda Forever*) have recently made the transition from streaming series to appearances in the main line of feature-length MCU films, and Feige has said that Miles Morales does exist in the primary world of the MCU, though he has yet to appear.

Bibliography

Adam (2018) 'Spider-Man Pointing at Spider-Man', *Know Your Meme*, online, 23 February, https://knowyourmeme.com/memes/spider-man-pointing-at-spider-man.

'All Miles Spider-Verse Suits – Spider-Man Miles Morales PC' (2023) online, *Flipdo*, 14 June, https://www.youtube.com/watch?v=csmPoQhc06M.

Avala, A. (2022) 'Why Sam Raimi's Spider-Man 4 Never Happened,' *Screen Rant*, online, 9 December, https://screenrant.com/why-spider-man-4-raimi-not-happen/.

Baldwin, J. (1985) *The Evidence of Things Not Seen*, New York: Henry Holt and Company.

Beck, J. (2018) 'The Trippy Columbia Logo Art in "Spider-Man: Into the Spider-Verse" ' *Cartoon Research*, online, 13 December, https://cartoonresearch.com/index.php/the-trippy-columbia-logo-art-in-spider-man-into-the-spiderverse/.

Belt, R. (2023) 'Writer Jason Reynolds on the Inner World of Miles Morales ,' *Marvel*, online, 19 May, https://www.marvel.com/articles/culture-lifestyle/miles-morales-suspended-a-spider-man-novel-this-week-in-marvel-interview-author-jason-reynolds.

Benhamou, E. (2022), *Contemporary Disney Animation: Genre, Gender and Hollywood*, Edinburgh: Edinburgh University Press.

Boffone, T. and Herrera, C. (2022) *Latinx Teens: Popular Culture on the Page, Stage and Screen*, Tucson, AZ: University of Arizona Press.

Bolter, J.D. and Grusin, R. (1999) *Remediation: Understanding New Media*, Cambridge, MA: MIT Press.

Boot, W. (2017) 'Exclusive: Sony Hack Reveals Studio's Detailed Plans for Another Spider-Man Reboot, ' *Daily Beast*, online, 14 April, https://www.thedailybeast.com/exclusive-sony-hack-reveals-studios-detailed-plans-for-another-spider-man-reboot.

Booth, P. and Williams, R. (eds) (2021) *A Fan Studies Primer: Method, Research, Ethics*, Iowa City, IA: University of Iowa Press.

Bordwell, D. (2006) *The Way Hollywood Tells It: Story and Style in Modern Movies.* Berkeley, CA: University of California Press.

Bowman, E. and Garcia-Navarro, L. (2019) 'Peter Ramsey Put the 1st Afro-Latino Spider-Man on Screen. It May Win Him an Oscar,' *Cap Radio,* online, 24 February, https://www.capradio.org/news/npr/story?storyid=697117295.

Branigan, E. (1982) *Point of View in the Cinema: A Theory of Narration and Subjectivity in Classic Film,* New York, NY: Mouton Publishers.

Breznican, A. (2021) 'Oscar Winner Peter Ramsey's Life Story Could Be Its Own Movie,' *Vanity Fair,* online, 16 April, https://www.vanityfair.com/hollywood/2021/04/peter-ramsey-spider-man-into-the-spider-verse-oscars.

Brinker, F. (2022) *Superhero Blockbusters: Seriality and Politics,* Edinburgh: Edinburgh University Press.

Brinker, F. (2017) 'Transmedia Storytelling in the "Marvel Cinematic Universe" and the Logics of Convergence Era Seriality' in M. Yockey (ed) *Make Ours Marvel: Media Convergence and a Comics Universe,* Austin, TX: University of Texas Press, pp. 207–234.

Brown, J.A. (2021) *Panthers, Hulks and Ironhearts: Marvel, Diversity and the 21st Century Superhero,* New Brunswick, NJ: Rutgers University Press.

Bui, H.-T. (2019) '"Spider-Man: Into the Spider-Verse" Deleted Scene Involved Miles' Roommate, Who Will Have a Bigger Part in the Sequel,' *Slash Film,* online, 7 January, https://www.slashfilm.com/563415/spider-man-into-the-spider-verse-deleted-scene-ganke-sequel/.

Bush, V. (1945) 'As We May Think', *The Atlantic Monthly* 176, pp. 101–108.

Castells, M. (1996) *The Rise of the Network Society,* London: Wiley-Blackwell.

Ching, A. (2015) 'Slott Details the Unexpected Origins of Spider-Gwen and Spider-Punk,' *CBR,* online, 11 March, https://www.cbr.com/slott-details-the-unexpected-origins-of-spider-gwen-and-spider-punk/.

Coogan P. (2006) *Superhero: The Secret Origins of a Genre,* New York, NY: MonkeyBrain Books.

Demby, G. (2012) 'LeBron James Tweets Picture of Miami Heat Wearing Hoodies in Solidarity with Family of Trayvon Martin,' *Huffington Post,* online, 23 March, https://www.huffpost.com/entry/lebron-heat-trayvon-tweet_n_1375831.

Dumas, M.J. and Nelson, J.D. (2016) '(Re)Imagining Black Boyhood: Toward a Critical Framework for Educational Research,' *Harvard Educational Review,* Vol. 86, No. 1, Spring, pp. 27–47.

DuVernay, A. (2019) 'Spider-Man: Into the Spider-Verse, Director Q&A,' *Sony Pictures Entertainment,* online, 14 February, https://www.youtube.com/watch?v=WvIphseK3pA.

Eco, U. (1985) '"Casablanca": Cult Movies and Intertextual Collage,' *SubStance,* Vol. 14, No. 2, pp. 3–12.

Eschoe, L. (2018), 'With #Blackboyjoy to Spare, Miles Morales is the Heart of the Spider-Verse,' *VoxAtl,* online, 19 December, https://voxatl.org/miles-morales-black-boy-joy/.

Fear, D. Hiatt, B., Sepinwall, A., Reeves, M., Gross, J. and Garrett, S. (2022) '50 Greatest Superhero Movies of All Time', *Rolling Stone*, 29 June, online, https://www.rollingstone.com/tv-movies/tv-movie-lists/greatest-superhero-m ovies-of-all-time-1367814.

Flegel, M. and Leggatt, J. (2021) *Superhero Culture Wars: Politics, Marketing, and Social Justice in Marvel Comics*, London: Bloomsbury.

Flood, M. (2021) *Moonlight: Screening Queer Black Youth*, London: Routledge.

Frank, K.M. (2016) 'Everybody Wants to Rule the Multiverse: Latino Spider-Man in Marvel's Media Empire' in F.L. Aldama and C. Gonzalez (eds) *Graphic Borders: Latino Comic Books Past, Present, and Future*, Austin, TX: University of Texas Press, pp. 241–252.

Genette, G. (1982) *Palimpsestes: La littérature au second degré*, Paris: Seuil.

Genette, G. (1997) *Palimpsests: Literature in the Second Degree*, Nebraska: University of Nebraska Press (C. Newman translator).

Gillespie, M.B. (2016) *Film Blackness: American Cinema and the Idea of Black Film*, Durham, NC: Duke University Press.

Gilmore, J.N. (2017) 'Spinning Webs: Constructing Authors, Genre, and Fans in the Spider-Man Film Franchise', in M. Yockey (ed) *Make Ours Marvel: Media Convergence and a Comics Universe*, Austin, TX: University of Texas Press, pp. 248–267.

Goodman, W. (2019) 'Breaking Down the Sony/Marvel Studios Spider-Man Deal – and What Went Wrong,' *Complex*, online, 21 August, https://www. complex.com/pop-culture/a/william-goodman/spider-man-sony-marvel-studios-deal-explained.

Gray, J. (2010) *Show Sold Separately: Promos, Spoilers and Other Media Paratexts*, New York, NY: New York University Press.

Gray, J., Sandvoss, C. and Harrington, C.L. (eds) (2017) *Fandom: Identities and Communities in a Mediated World*, London: Routledge.

Guerrero, E. (1993) *Framing Blackness: The African American Image in Film*, Philadelphia, PA: Temple University Press.

Guzman, F. (2023) 'Burger King Debuts Red Whopper Ahead of "Spider-Man: Across the Spider-Verse" Premiere' *USA Today*, online, 5 August, https://www.usatoday.com/story/money/food/2023/05/08/burger-king-sp ider-man-across-the-spider-verse-whopper/70195993007/.

Gvozden, D. (2018) 'A Definitive List of "Spider-Man: Into the Spider-Verse" Easter Eggs,' *Hollywood Reporter*, online, 14 December, https://www.holly woodreporter.com/movies/movie-videos/all-spider-man-spider-verse-easter-eggs-revealed-1169124/.

Hall, S. (1980) 'Encoding/Decoding,' in S. Hall, D. Hobson, A. Lowe, and P. Willis (eds) *Culture, Media, Language*, London: Hutchinson University Library, pp. 128–138.

Hall, S. (1997) 'Race: The Floating Signifier', Lecture Delivered at Goldsmiths College, *Media Education Foundation*, online https://www.mediaed.org/tra nscripts/Stuart-Hall-Race-the-Floating-Signifier-Transcript.pdf.

Hanna, A. (2021) 'The Clothes Make the (Spider) Man: Costumes and Identity in Spider-Man: Into the Spider-Verse', unpublished paper, Society for Cinema and Media Studies Conference.

Harris, H. (2019) 'Spider-Man: Into the Spider-Verse Had to Get You to Love Miles Morales in 45 Seconds', *Vulture*, online, 20 February, https://www.vulture.com/2019/02/how-spider-verse-got-you-to-love-miles-morales-in-45-seconds.html.

Hassler-Forrest, D. (2017) 'The Politics of World-Building: Heteroglossia in Janelle Monáe's Afro-Futurist WondaLand,' in M. Boni (ed) *World-Building: Transmedia, Fans, Industries*, Amsterdam: University of Amsterdam Press, pp. 377–391.

Hastings, C. (2022) *How to Read Comics the Marvel Way*, New York, NY: Outreach/New Reader.

Higgins, S. (2016) *Matinee Melodrama: Playing with Formula in the Sound Serial*, New Brunswick, NJ: Rutgers University Press.

Hills, M. (2002) *Fan Cultures*, London: Routledge.

Holmon, O. (no date a) 'Spider-Man #2 Review', *Black Nerd Problems*, online, https://blacknerdproblems.com/spider-man-2-review/.

Holmon, O. (no date b) 'Miles Morales vs. Spider-Man: When You and Your Blackness Disagree,' *Black Nerd Problems*, online, https://blacknerdproblems.com/miles-morales-vs-spider-man-when-you-and-your-blackness-disagree/.

'How Animators Created the Spider-Verse,' (2019) *Wired*, online, 22 March, https://www.youtube.com/watch?v=l-wUKu_V2Lk.

'How "Spider-Man: Into the Spider-Verse" Was Animated' (2019) *Movies Insider*, online, 21 February, https://www.youtube.com/watch?v=jEXUG_vN540&t=134s.

Houdek, M. (2018) 'The Imperative of Race for Rhetorical Studies: Toward Divesting from Disciplinary and Institutionalized Whiteness', *Communication and Critical/Cultural Studies*, Vol. 15, No. 4, pp. 292–299.

Hutcheon, L. (2012) *A Theory of Adaptation*, 2nd edition, New York, NY: Routledge.

Jackson, M. (2006) 'The Enthymematic Hegemony of Whiteness: The Enthymeme as Anti-Racist Rhetorical Strategy,' *JRC*, Vol. 26, No. 3/4, pp. 601–641.

'James Gunn Ranks Spider-Man: Into the Spider-Verse as the Greatest Superhero Movie'(2023) *GQ*, online, 16 May, https://www.youtube.com/watch?v=UZ7MdgP9PKE.

Jeffries, D. (2022) '"Anyone Can Wear the Mask": The Marginalization of Miles Morales in *Spider-Man: Into the Spider-Verse*"', *JCMS* Vol. 62, No. 5, pp. 192–214.

Jeffries, D. (2017) *Comic Book Film Style: Cinema at 24 Panels per Second*, Austin, TX: University of Texas Press.

Jenkins, H. (2017) 'Remediating Comics for Cinema: An Interview with Drew Morton (Part Three),' *Pop Junctions: Reflections on Entertainment, Pop Culture, Activism, Media Literacy, Fandom and More*, online, 3 April, http://

henryjenkins.org/blog/2017/04/remediating-comics-for-cinema-an-interview-with-drew-morton-part-three.html.

Jenkins, H. (2009), 'The Revenge of the Origami Unicorn: Seven Principles of Transmedia Storytelling', *Pop Junctions: Reflections on Entertainment, Pop Culture, Activism, Media Literacy, Fandom and More*, online, 12 December, http://henryjenkins.org/blog/2009/12/the_revenge_of_the_origami_uni.html.

Jenkins, H. (2007), 'Transmedia Storytelling 101', *Pop Junctions: Reflections on Entertainment, Pop Culture, Activism, Media Literacy, Fandom and More*, online, 21 March, http://henryjenkins.org/blog/2007/03/transmedia_storytelling_101.html.

Jenkins, H. (2006) *Convergence Culture: Where Old and New Media Collide.* New York, NY: New York University Press.

Jenkins, H. (1992) *Textual Poachers: Television Fans and Participatory Culture,* London: Routledge.

Jenkins, H., Shresthova, S., Gamber-Thompson, L., Kligler-Vilenchik, N. and Zimmerman, A. (2009) *By Any Media Necessary: The New Youth Activism,* New York, NY: New York University Press.

Johnson, D. (2017) 'Battleworlds: The Management of Multiplicity in the Media Industries,' in M. Boni (ed) *World Building. Transmedia, Fans, Industries,* Amsterdam: Amsterdam UP, pp. 129–142.

Johnson, D. (2013) *Media Franchising: Creative License and Collaboration in the Culture Industries,* New York, NY: New York University Press.

Johnson, D. (2012) 'Cinematic Destiny: Marvel Studios and the Industrial Histories of Media Convergence,' *Cinema Journal*, Vol. 52, No. 1, pp. 1–24.

Kawin, B. (1978) *Mindscreen: Bergman, Godard and First-Person Film.* Princeton, NJ: Princeton University Press.

Keane, S. (2020) 'Marvel's "Spider-Man: Miles Morales" Is the Perfect PS5 Launch Title,' *CNET*, online, 12 November, https://www.cnet.com/culture/marvels-spider-man-miles-morales-is-the-perfect-ps5-launch-title/.

Klinger, B. (2006), *Beyond the Multiplex: Cinema, New Technologies, and the Home,* Berkeley, CA: University of California Press.

Latour, J. (2022) 'Understanding Kirby Crackle', *The Drawl*, online, 22 August, https://www.youtube.com/watch?v=aQZb9uSepx8.

Labonte, R. (2020) 'Spider-Man: Into the Spider-Verse Writer Reveals Complex Rewriting Process,' *Screen Rant*, online, 22 March, https://screenrant.com/spiderman-spiderverse-phil-lord-rewriting-process/.

Lévy, P. (1999) *Collective Intelligence: Mankind's Emerging World in Cyberspace,* Cambridge: Perseus Books (R. Bonnano, translator).

McCloud, S. (2006) *Making Comics: Storytelling Secrets of Comics, Manga, and Graphic Novels,* New York, NY: William Morrow Paperbacks.

McCloud, S. (2000) *Reinventing Comics: The Evolution of an Art Form,* New York, NY: William Morrow Paperbacks.

McCloud, S. (1994) *Understanding Comics: The Invisible Art,* New York, NY: William Morrow Paperbacks.

McKelly, J..C. (2008) 'The Double Truth, Ruth: Do the Right Thing and the Culture of Ambiguity' in *The Spike Lee Reader*, ed. P. Massood, Philadelphia, PA: Temple UP, 58–76.

Meikle, K. (2019) *Adaptations in the Franchised Era: 2001–16*, New York, NY: Bloomsbury Academic.

Meeuf, R. (2021) 'Fighting Against the Spider-Verse: The Kingpin and Hyperwhite Villainy,' unpublished paper, Society for Cinema and Media Studies Conference.

Minett, M. and Schauer, B. (2017) 'Reforming the "Justice" System: Marvel's Avengers and the Transformation of the All-Star Team Book' in M. Yockey (ed) *Make Ours Marvel: Media Convergence and a Comics Universe*, Austin, TX: University of Texas Press, pp. 39–65.

Mittell, J. (2015) *Complex TV: The Poetics of Contemporary Television Storytelling*, New York, NY: New York University Press.

Mittell, J. (2012), 'Forensic Fandom and the Drillable Text,' *Pop Junctions: Reflections on Entertainment, Pop Culture, Activism, Media Literacy, Fandom and More*, online, 17 December, https://henryjenkins.org/blog/2012/12/more-spreadable-media-rethinking-transmedia-engagement.html.

Molina-Guzmán, I. (2021) 'Into the Spider-Verse and the Commodified Re-Imagining of Afro-Rican Visibility' in S.A. Dagbovie-Mullins and E.L. Berlatsky (eds) *Mixed-Race Superheroes*, Lewisburg, PA: Bucknell University Press, pp. 220–243.

Molloy, T. (2018) 'Let's Talk About the Seamless Racial Cues of Into the Spider-Verse,' (Episode 18 'The Low Key Racial Subtext of "Into the Spider-Verse"') *The Wrap*, online, 24 December, https://www.thewrap.com/into-the-spider-verse-low-key-beautiful-racial-subtext-podcast/.

Morton, D. (2016) *Panel to Screen: Style, American Film, and Comic Books during the Blockbuster Era*, Jackson, MS: University of Mississippi Press.

Murray, J. (1997) *Hamlet on the Holodeck: The Future of Narrative in Cyberspace*, Cambridge, MA: MIT Press.

Muzdakas, M. (2022) *'The Original Photo that Inspired the Iconic Columbia Pictures "Torch Lady" Logo,'* *My Modern Met*, online, 21 February, https://mymodernmet.com/torch-photo-columbia-pictures/.

O'Connell, S. (2022) *With Great Power: How Spider-Man Conquered Hollywood During the Golden Age of Comic Book Blockbusters*. Essex, CT: Applause Theater & Cinema Books.

Pande, R. (2020) *Fandom, Now in Color: A Collection of Voices*, Iowa City, IA: University of Iowa Press.

Perren, A. and Steirer, G. (2021), *The American Comic Book Industry and Hollywood*, London: British Film Institute.

Raymond, C.N. (2023) 'The Origin of the Spider-Man Pointing Meme,' *Screen Rant*, online, 3 July, https://screenrant.com/spider-man-pointing-meme-cartoon-origin/.

Reid, M. (1993) *Redefining Black Film*, Berkely, CA: University of California Press.

Renfro, K. (2020) '"Spider-Man: Into the Spider-Verse" Directors Confirm a Fan Theory about This Small Detail You Might Have Missed in the Movie's

Most Triumphant Scene,'*Insider*, online, 17 November, https://www.insider.com/spider-verse-miles-breaking-glass-theory-2019-2.

Reynolds, J. (2023) *Miles Morales: Suspended: A Spider-Man Novel*, NY: Simon and Schuster.

Reynolds, J. (2017) *Miles Morales: Spider-Man*, New York, NY: Marvel Press.

Richards, D. (2017) 'Interview: Miles Morales Web Slings into the World of Prose,' *CBR*, 23 August, online, https://www.cbr.com/interview-miles-morales-novel-jason-reynolds/.

Robinson, J. (2018) 'Sony Finally Untangles Its Spider Web,' *Vanity Fair*, online, 14 December, https://www.vanityfair.com/hollywood/2018/12/sony-spider-man-future-amy-pascal-phil-lord-interview.

Ryan, M-L. (2013) 'Transmedial Storytelling and Transfictionality,' *Poetics Today*, Vol. 34, No. 3, pp. 361–388.

Scolari, C.A. (2019) 'Networks: From Text to Hypertext, Publishing to Sharing, and Single Author to Collaborative Production,' in A. Phillips and M. Bhaskar (eds) *The Oxford Handbook of Publishing*, Oxford: Oxford University Press, pp. 127–146.

Scott, S. and Click, M. (eds) (2017) *The Routledge Companion to Media Fandom*, London: Routledge.

Sexton, J. (2017) *Black Masculinity and the Cinema of Policing*, London: Palgrave Macmillan.

Snyder, C. (2019) 'How Oscar-Winning "Spider-Man: Into the Spider-Verse" Changed Comic Book Movies Forever,' *Business Insider*, online, 25 February, https://www.businessinsider.com/spiderman-spider-man-into-spider-verse-animated-frame-rate-marvel-stan-lee-2019-2?r=US&IR=T.

Sobchack, V. (1992) *The Address of the Eye: A Phenomenology of Film Experience*, Princeton, NJ: Princeton University Press.

'"Spider-Man: Into the Spider-Verse" Concept Art by Alberto Mielgo' (no date) *Concept ArtWorld*, online, https://conceptartworld.com/news/spider-man-into-the-spider-verse-concept-art-by-alberto-mielgo/.

'*Spider-Man: Across the Spider-Verse* Review (Spoiler Free)' (2023) *Amazing Spider-Talk Podcast*, online, 1 June, https://www.youtube.com/watch?v=FWGrkjCKoYk.

'Spider-Man AnimatedMovie Coming in 2018' *(2015) Variety*, online, 22 April, https://variety.com/2015/film/news/spider-man-animated-movie-coming-in-2018-1201477933/.

'Spider-Man Remastered vs. Spider-Man: Miles Morales – Physics and Details Comparison' (2023), *GameBest*, online, 7 January, https://www.youtube.com/watch?v=wJ-3ztd4ULA&t=22s.

'Spiderverse Look Tutorial' (2019) *Ina*, online, 2 March, https://www.youtube.com/watch?v=97HJTsiMdnM.

Stam, R. (2000) 'Beyond Fidelity: The Dialogics of Adaptation' in J. Naremore (ed) *Film Adaptation*, New Brunswick, NJ: Rutgers University Press, pp. 54–76.

Summers, S. (2019) 'Adapting a Retro Comic Aesthetic with Spider-Man: Into the Spider-Verse', *Adaptation*, Vol. 12, No. 2, pp. 190–194.

Taylor, J.C. (2021a) 'Reading the Marvel Cinematic Universe: The Avengers' Intertextual Aesthetic,' *JCMS*, Vol. 60, No. 3, pp. 129–156.

Taylor, J.C. (2021b) 'Postmodern Parody in Animated Superhero Cinema' in L. Piatti-Farnell (ed) *The Superhero Multiverse: Readapting Comic Book Icons in Twenty-First Century Film and Popular Media*, Lanham, MD: Lexington Books, pp. 87–104.

'The Secrets Behind Spider-Man: Into the Spider-Verse with Phil Lord and Chris Miller: On Animation ' (2019) *BAFTA Guru*, online, 15 July, https://www.youtube.com/watch?v=Ub-g7guuQgY.

Weiner, R.G. and Peaslee, R.M. (2012) 'Introduction' in R. Weiner and R.M. Peaslee (eds) *Web-Spinning Heroics: Critical Essays on the History and Meaning of Spider-Man*, Jefferson, NC: McFarland, pp. 4–21.

'"What's Up Danger" Scene Recreation Into the Spider-Verse (Spider-Man PS5)' (2022), *ItlsSpd*, online, 8 January, https://www.youtube.com/watch?v=mYiZNvdsTF8.

Wolf, M.J.P. (2012) *Building Imaginary Worlds: The Theory and History of Subcreation*, New York, NY: Routledge.

Wong, W. and Malone, K. (2022) 'The Spider-Man Problem,' *Planet Money*, podcast, *NPR*, 28 January, online, https://www.npr.org/transcripts/1076531156.

Worlds, M. and Miller, H. (2019) 'Miles Morales: Spider-Man and Reimagining the Canon for Racial Justice,' *English Journal*, Vol. 108, No. 4, pp. 43–50.

Xendi, I. (2020) 'Introduction' in J. Reynolds *Stamped: Racism, Antiracism, and You*, New York, NY: Little, Brown Books for Young Readers, pp. ix–xvi.

Xendi, I. (2016) *Stamped from the Beginning: The Definitive History of Racist Ideas in America*, New York, NY: Bold Type Books.

Index

Note: page numbers in *italics* indicate a figure.

For Product Safety Concerns and Information please contact our EU
representative GPSR@taylorandfrancis.com
Taylor & Francis Verlag GmbH, Kaufingerstraße 24, 80331 München, Germany